A TRAVELLER PASSING THROUGH

A TRAVELLER PASSING THROUGH

Reflections from the Holy Land

Ruth Patterson

VERITAS

Published 2022 by
Veritas Publications
7–8 Lower Abbey Street
Dublin 1
Ireland
publications@veritas.ie
www.veritas.ie

ISBN 978 1 80097 016 8

All biblical quotations come from The Holy Bible, New Living Translation.

10 9 8 7 6 5 4 3 2 1

A catalogue record for this book is available from the British Library.

Designed by Jeannie Swan, Veritas Publications
Printed in the Republic of Ireland by SPRINT-print Ltd, Dublin

Veritas Publications is a member of Publishing Ireland.

Veritas books are printed on paper made from the wood pulp of managed forests. For every tree felled, at least one tree is planted, thereby renewing natural resources.

CONTENTS

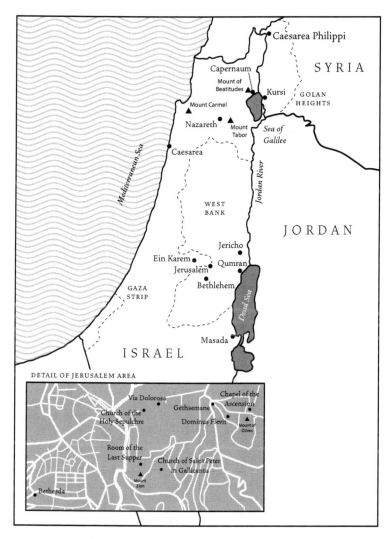

A map of the Holy Land showing the principal places mentioned in this book

INTRODUCTION

IN JUNE 2018, I WAS INVITED TO BE PART OF A GROUP OF people who were going on pilgrimage to the Holy Land. I had never been before, although there had been three previous abortive attempts – for various reasons, the plans for each of these tours had collapsed during the preparatory stages. So when this opportunity presented itself, and showed no signs of being withdrawn, it seemed as if the time was finally right and that this was meant to be. The invitation was to go and simply absorb the experience, with the possibility of writing about it on my return. The opportunity to do that had not fully presented itself until now. As the time between the visit and the actual writing of this book has lengthened, the impressions have only become clearer rather than blurred, certain irrelevancies have faded, and I can 'see, hear, touch, taste and smell' the essence of what, for me, has become one of the most remarkable journeys of my life. This is why, throughout these pages, I tend to reflect in the present tense. The journey was never merely a physical one: it was also a profoundly spiritual one. It was never merely an external pilgrimage but, much more challenging, an inner one as well. And that journey continues.

As a pilgrim, I was forcibly reminded of a verse from Psalm 39, 'I am your guest, a traveller passing through, as my ancestors were before me'; hence the title of this book. We were not so much the guests of a particular country but of the Spirit and, in that sense, we were travelling on holy ground. I love this story of Columba, my favourite Irish saint. A traveller was visiting him in his cell on the island of Iona. He looked around at the bareness of the saint's cell.

'Where's your furniture?'

'Where's yours?' responded Columba.

'Mine?' said the traveller. 'But I'm just passing through.'

'So am I,' replied Columba.

This was brought home to me at the very start of our trip when the only set of luggage not to turn up at Ben Gurion Airport in Tel Aviv was mine. At the outset I felt that God was challenging me to let go; to let go of some of the things I felt were essentials and so important; to let go of my preconceived ideas about people and places and simply to be present and open. Incidentally, the luggage did eventually turn up, twenty-four hours later!

The sites we visited during our pilgrimage are marked indelibly on my mind. They became for me places of encounter. Some of these are what I want to share with you in this book, not in any biblical, chronological order and not necessarily in the sequence in which we actually visited them, either, but rather as these places spoke to me, or whispered to me, in unexpected moments. With each chapter we will visit a number of places that seemed to be linked together in these whispers that took me unawares. I hope that you will enjoy travelling with me and that these reflections will also become places of encounter for you. Perhaps we can all let go a little, be more aware, more open to the eternal 'now' that throbs with presence wherever we happen to be in this world. So let us 'board the coach' and begin our pilgrimage. Welcome to the Holy Land!

CHAPTER ONE

SEE WHAT'S NOT THERE

Caesarea Maritima;
Qumran; Masada

(Ecclesiastes 3:1–15)

IT IS THE FIRST FULL DAY OF OUR PILGRIMAGE IN ISRAEL.
We have spent the night in Netanya, near Tel Aviv.
Because my luggage is still in the airport at Istanbul, I
have had to rely on borrowed necessities. But this is a new
day, the sun is shining from a cloudless sky and everyone
is eagerly anticipating our drive along the Mediterranean
coastline where we will get our first taste of what is in
store for us over the next ten days. We will be stopping at
Caesarea Maritima, Haifa and Acre. I forget all about my
lost luggage and allow myself to be overtaken by a sense
of wonder and gratitude at actually being here. Our tour
organiser, our local guide and our spiritual accompanier
have many riches to share with us. There is a great buzz in
the coach as people talk excitedly to each other. Some of
them have been to the Holy Land before but, for most of
us, it's our first time. Our spiritual accompanier has given
us good advice: he challenges us to see what's not there.
In other words, he wants us to use our imaginations to

bring to life what was once a living, vibrant world. His words will become a mantra for the entire trip. As I begin to share my memories with you, dear reader, I find myself going back to the site we visited on that very first day and, in my mind's eye, I see it clearly and hear again some of the conversation.

This first site is Caesarea Maritima, where we are invited to appreciate the power of Rome and to picture the ruins restored to their former glory. All around us are unmistakable signs of one-time greatness. Of strategic importance as a seaport, and as principal residence of the Roman Procurators of Judea, Caesarea Maritima is impressive. Developed by that gifted madman Herod the Great, in honour of the 'Emperor of the whole world', Caesar Augustus, everywhere we look we see ruined signs of wealth and power. Palace, arena, amphitheatre, temple, statues, storehouses, aqueduct, harbour: all convey the pride and self-belief that this empire would last forever. 'Kingdoms come and kingdoms go,' my companion murmurs. It is true. We happen on the remains of an inscription by Pontius Pilate in reference to a building erected in honour of the emperor Tiberius. I try to see what's not there. I see someone who is remembered through history, not for buildings or military prowess or great leadership but as the one who washed his hands, who 'allowed' Jesus to be crucified. Already I am captivated by a sense of past becoming present.

I look around and, in my imagination, 'see' another Roman, a centurion called Cornelius, revered for his faith in God and for his generosity, the first Gentile to be welcomed through baptism into the fledgling Christian Church. Peter the Apostle comes to Caesarea after a time of prayer and fasting in which his understanding of who belongs in God's kingdom and who does not was stretched way beyond the limits of his faith and culture. Inspired by an encounter with Cornelius, Peter pleads the case for those outside the Jewish faith to be accepted as followers of the Way. Inclusion becomes the order of the day. I 'look' again and a third Roman emerges: Paul, a citizen of the Roman Empire by birth, the great apostle to the Gentiles, who first brought the Good News to Europe. Here in Caesarea he was held prisoner for two years before being transported to Rome where he eventually met his death. I see in this place what is no longer here. The once vast empire of Rome is no more than crumbling buildings and ancient artefacts to be marvelled at as we pay a nodding tribute to a bygone culture that once believed itself invincible.

Some days later, we board the coach for what we have been told will be a long day. I am intrigued because we are visiting two places that are not really overtly mentioned in Scripture. Our coach brings us from Jerusalem to below sea level, en route to Masada, the famous fortress/palace created by Herod the Great. But we stop first at Qumran, on the north-west shore of the Dead Sea. Why?

Muhammed edh-Dhib, a young Bedouin goatherd, would never have been heard of had he not, one day in 1947, missed one of his flock and thrown a stone into a cave in an effort to find it. The impact of the stone made an unusual sound. Later searches revealed eight earthenware jars containing ancient writings, part of what we now call the Dead Sea Scrolls. This amazing discovery included copies of nearly all the Old Testament books and a scroll of the rules governing the strict local Essene community. The missing goat had opened up a world and a way of life long since forgotten. We are all eager to explore what remains of the community who lived here about two thousand years ago.

We need to take some time to appreciate how miraculous was the goatherd's accidental discovery among the myriad small caves that pockmark the steep sandy cliffs, and to learn something of the isolated religious sect, widely believed to be a branch of the Essenes, which inhabited this desolate place off and on for over two hundred years. In sweltering temperatures of over 40°C, we retreat to an air-conditioned room to watch a video reconstruct for us their day-to-day routine that adhered strictly to the principles of poverty, chastity, obedience and a strictly controlled community life. We then emerge to walk around some of the reclaimed ruins. Once again, I try to see what's not there. Most fascinating to me is the Scriptorium where the community painstakingly copied the manuscripts that are now such priceless treasures.

Little did they know when they placed their work in jars and hid them in the caves just on the cusp of the final conquest of Judea by the Romans in AD 70 that these same scrolls would not see the light of day for over nineteen hundred years!

I realise that it would take someone far more knowledgeable and learned than me to grasp a true picture of this people's beliefs, practices and motivations. I think about this group of people who removed themselves from the ordinary life of their day and who practised such exclusion and asceticism in order to be pure and to fulfil all righteousness by observing so many rituals and regulations. True, they left a valuable legacy in the recovered scrolls, but what else? Did they become aware in the end that they were part of a common humanity, broken and beloved, that will never be 'perfect' and 'pure' in the way to which they committed? Or did they die with their beliefs intact?

I reflect that throughout history there have been people who have committed to a similar way of life, striving to be perfect, to be pure. In order to do this, they have observed innumerable rules and regulations that, I imagine, were never enough to satisfy either them or their fellows. Such practices, unless accompanied by a transformative inner journey, can lead to the sort of behaviour that Jesus condemned so strongly in many of the Pharisees of his day. But I also reflect on the many who, down the centuries, have removed themselves from the distractions of the world to live in enclosed communities in order to devote themselves to a life of prayer. Their motivation is that of love – love for God and for his creation, including humankind. In that sense, they remain in the world yet not of it. I believe that their faithful, praying presence, their awareness of that spiritual dimension, their surrender to mystery, their letting go and letting 'God be God' contribute more than we will ever know to restoring this wonderful, anguished, shining, terrible, beloved earth. I wonder if I am being fair to these ancient Essenes in assuming that their lives were more about striving than about being. Perhaps I am. On reflection, I am sure that among their ranks there were elements of both, but I do not know.

Not for the first time, what I do recognise as I wander around these ruins is that I, too, have within me both tendencies. There is a sizeable part of me that likes order, that feels safe when I see the way ahead mapped out to the last detail, when there are rules to follow and rituals to observe. I can relax and be more comfortable. While this 'comfort' may, in fact, at times feel uncomfortable, it takes a lot to shake me out of it. It is, perhaps, because it makes me feel more in control. When the urge comes to entertain the notion that there could be another way of looking at things, another as yet unexplored route to follow that would lead me to that deeper relationship with God for which my being yearns, my first instinct is probably to repress or dismiss it. I turn my attention to working harder at the familiar, striving to observe the pattern laid down with greater intensity. There is a tendency in many of us to strive to protect the ego, the smaller self, at all costs. Of course, we all need our smaller selves in order to function day to day. But deeper than that is the whisper that can take us unawares, from beyond us or deep within us, of something more, of discovering more of our true selves and, in so doing, of discovering more of God. Such a quest will lead us into unknown territory, into the realm of mystery that partially explains our resistance; better to try a little bit harder, to strive a little bit more with what we know, than to risk letting go. Actually, whenever I do take time to stand back, to reflect, to simply be, I see how crazy it is to think that my little earnest strivings to defend my always fragile ego or smaller self could hold back that infinite love that is continually directing its gaze on me. Such a quest urges me to come down on the side of my true self, to have the courage to recognise the light within. It is to acknowledge, not just in my head but from the depths of my being, that I am a child of God, broken and beloved, and to be open to going, and to being, where that leads me. It is to dare to dream and then to keep on seeking, in trust, to incarnate that dream.

I wonder again about these ancient 'monks'. In their quest for purity and perfection, did they sometimes hear the divine whisper of 'something more'? Did they ever get a glimpse of that spiritual dimension throbbing with infinite love? Did they, in their desire to be pure and perfect, resist the call to relationship, a call that would inevitably have led them into mystery? Did they ever allow themselves to feel the love and suffering that can be the catalyst for transformation? Did they ever embrace the notion of a universe created in love and for love? Did they come to the end of their days, especially in the latter days of their existence at Qumran so soon to be scattered, wiped out by the conquering Roman forces, with a sense of failure and despair or with a flash of awareness of the vast open spaces of God's love and mercy that awaits them on the next mysterious stage of their journey?

As we make our way back to the coach to continue to Masada, my mind leaps to my own land of Ireland where, about fifteen hundred years ago, the Irish monks also 'lived community', followed monastic rules and worked long hours in the Scriptorium, copying the Gospels and the Psalms. The contrast with the Essenes is sharp – the Irish monks were inclusive. They opened their hearts to embrace a broken and imperfect world of which they were a part, a world full of diversity yet recognised by them as totally connected, inter-related and sacred, a world that needed to hear the promise and the hope of the words they were copying. So they became pilgrims, voyagers, explorers, adventurers; often exiles. They set out, not really knowing where they were going but trusting their destinations to the God who had placed his mark of loving ownership upon them; people like Colmcille, Brendan, Brigid, Columbanus and countless others, bearers of the Word, image-bearers of hope, icons of faith to strange and unfamiliar places and peoples. Their legacy not only survives but is a living, vibrant thing that still today pinpoints and illumines that spiritual dimension which is the ultimate reality.

Our spiritual accompanier's challenge to see what's not there has been effective but has left me in a somewhat sombre mood as we drive away. I would not want to unfairly criticise these upright, worthy men who were acting according to the light they had been given – and I must not forget the wonderful legacy of the scrolls. I return to the present moment and fix my eyes on the passing landscape – dry, arid desert, with little sign of life, although my informed common sense tells me that every desert teems with life, even if largely invisible. Long before we arrive at the base of Masada, the famous rock fortress near the shores of the Dead Sea, we see it rising out of the desert, separated from other hills and cliffs, solitary and mysterious, like the stories it holds. Throughout my life, I have been a great lover of poetry. Phrases or whole verses often spring to mind, arising from some vast, half-forgotten well of words, and connect with the present moment. Today it happens again. Percy Bysshe Shelley's sonnet 'Ozymandias' speaks to me as clearly as when I first studied it as a schoolgirl. Ozymandias was the Greek name of an ancient, powerful Pharoah of Egypt, Rameses II. Shelley had seen, in the British Museum, a fragment of a massive sculpture of this once seemingly unassailable tyrant dating from the thirteenth century BC, found in the desert. All that is left are 'two vast and trunkless legs of stone', a 'shattered visage' and a broken pedestal on which appear the still legible words:

My name is Ozymandias, King of Kings;
Look on my works, ye Mighty, and despair!

Shelley concludes his sonnet that reflects on the ravages of time, of history littered with the ruins of past glories, and the temporary nature of even the most powerful tyrant's influence, with these words:

Nothing beside remains. Round the decay
Of that colossal wreck, boundless and bare
The lone and distant sands stretch far away.*

As we step out of the coach, the heat hits us, fierce in its intensity. Our way up is by cable car, giving us a panoramic view and an appreciation of how arduous the climb would have been by foot. At the top is a far-reaching plateau where we explore just some of the two-thousand-year-old feats of engineering that made this place virtually impregnable. It was not only unassailable but also luxurious. The creativity behind such an ambitious project was largely that of Herod the Great, who died in AD 4. This is the same monarch who was so consumed with mistrust of anyone or anything that might smack of rivalry that he murdered his wife, Mariamne, and other members of his family. Among the other nefarious deeds for which he is deemed responsible was the Slaughter of the Innocents, recorded in Matthew, Chapter 2. He did, however, have a zeal for building and there are relics of his enterprises in many different parts of this land.

Masada seems to be the one that attracts the most interest and is surrounded by so many stories that it is difficult to separate myth from historical fact. What is beyond dispute, and what is so poignantly and zealously remembered to this day, is the last stand made here in AD 73 against the Romans by nearly one thousand Sicarii, a splinter group of the Zealots, a Jewish sect. This rock fortress seemed unassailable. It gave the Sicarii solid protection and a good lifestyle, so carefully had Herod planned its water supply, its grain stores, its wines and fruits, its baths and leisure facilities, its well-supplied weapon stores. The Sicarii held out for about three years. It was only after the Romans, under their commander Lucius Flavius Silva, built enormous ramps and introduced mighty battering rams that the fortress dwellers knew the end had come. On the eve of the Roman ascent, they planned and executed a mass suicide directed by their leader, Eleazar ben Ya'ir. I have always been rather morbidly fascinated by this, after picking up David Kossoff's *Voices of Masada*,** a novel based on a report by the first-century Romano-Jewish historian

Flavius Josephus that five children and two women had escaped to tell the story, so that it would never be forgotten.

It certainly has never been forgotten. In spite of the heat, the cloudless sky, the clear evidence of intricate planning and the amazing feats of engineering, the stark beauty all around and stretching into the distance, I sense the shadow that hangs over this place. What people remember, what I will remember, is not so much Herod's brilliant, inventive mind but this one story of Masada's end. Perhaps it is the whispered voices of the dead that accompany us down the mountain, creating a more sombre, reflective mood. As we descend and find our coach (in which the air conditioning has temporarily broken down!), words and phrases flit through my mind: waste, inhumanity, cruelty, not learning from our history, the glorification of military power and of armed resistance. This is not to single out this land but rather to reflect on the many peoples throughout history who have followed a similar route in seeking to build something lasting, not on the solid rock of truth and justice and mercy, but on the blood of innocents – and on the belief that God (whatever god they worshipped) was on their side. The poignancy for me is due to the fact that where I come from – Ireland – is no exception.

As our coach speeds back to Jerusalem, we are weary from the heat, the long day and all the conflicting emotions associated with old, unhappy, far-off things. But I am thankful that, in our packed schedule, our pilgrimage has included these places, Caesarea Maritima, Qumran and Masada. The once invincible Roman Empire, the mad tyranny and genius of Herod the Great – these have been lost in the sands of time. They are truly ruins in the desert. Even the devotion and earnest work of the Essenes have faded. But I am also supremely thankful for the challenge to see what's not there; as the writer of Ecclesiastes reminds us, there is a time for everything, but even as things pass, one thing remains. As we near our hotel for the night, I 'see' a different kingdom whose citizens come from every race and tribe and tongue of whom our little group of pilgrims are a part. True, they are held together by power, but it is the power of love. The hallmarks of this kingdom are mercy, justice, truth and peace. Its all-pervading power and influence are largely hidden but I know it will outlast all others and be there at the end of time itself.

---

* Percy Bysshe Shelley, 'Ozymandias' in Louis Untermeyer (ed.), *The Albatross Book of Living Verse* (London: W. Collins Sons and Co. Ltd.), p. 350.

** David Kossoff, *Voices of Masada* (London: Fount Paperbacks, 1983).

Do you ever find yourself being stretched
beyond the limits of your own faith,
tradition and culture? If not, why not?

Thank you, Lord, for those who have
painstakingly and courageously preserved
the Scriptures for us. Help us to value
their work by living the Word.

Thank you for the qualities of zeal,
commitment and loyalty. May they always
be tempered by mercy and used to build
up rather than pull down. Amen.

CHAPTER TWO

WHO IS JESUS?

Caesarea Philippi;
Sea of Galilee

*(Matthew 16:13–20;
John 21:1–23)*

EACH DAY OUR LITTLE GROUP OF ABOUT TWENTY
pilgrims boards the coach early in the morning, long
before the sun is high in the sky. There is a sense of
anticipation; excitement, even. What will this day
bring? What encounters will surprise us? What new
awareness will be ours? Today the coach takes us north,
driving along by the Golan Heights to the region of
Caesarea Philippi. It was here that Jesus asked his
disciples the question that halted them in their tracks
and that still today arrests our attention and compels
us to reflect on our answer. 'What are people saying
about me?' It is the first question, one that we, like
the disciples, have no difficulty in responding to. You
can imagine how it was. Eager to encourage him, they
chipped in with 'John the Baptist, Elijah or one of the
other great Prophets.' But then Jesus asked another
question. There was a pause, not an empty pause
but one that was vibrant, pregnant with expectancy,

apprehension, fear, mystery, unknowing. 'What about you? Who do you say I am?'

This question is to the forefront of my mind as we leave the comfort of the coach and begin our ascent in the searing heat. We find ourselves standing midway between two points. On one side is one of the three main sources of the River Jordan, a stream flowing from Mount Hermon. On the other is a cliff face, pockmarked with caves and various altars to pagan gods. One cave is very large and, before shifts occurred in the rock formation, was the source of the spring that now flows below where we have stopped. In pagan belief, this was an entrance to the Underworld, known as the Gates of Hell. It was believed that the Underworld was surrounded by five rivers, denoting woe, lamentation, fire, forgetfulness and oath-taking. These rivers separated the living from the dead. There is in this place, in spite of the heat, a sense of foreboding, of darkness, of death; human sacrifices were offered here to the god Pan. We are standing between the source of life – the headwaters of the Jordan – and the threatening shapes of Hades. My companion, who is quick to pick up on the atmosphere, moves away. She cannot remain too long in such a place.

It was here that Jesus' question broke through the ominous silence; the oppressive atmosphere. 'Who do you say I am?' There was a pause. Jesus waited. His friends were uncomfortable, perhaps shifting from one foot to the other, looking at the ground, not daring to meet the eyes of their comrades, let alone the eyes of Jesus. How should they respond? Jesus' words hung in the air between them. This was the most important question they would ever be asked. Peter, as usual, jumped in where others feared to tread and declared, 'You are the Messiah, the Son of the Living God!' The heart of Jesus rejoiced and he responded, 'Blessed are you, Simon son of John. And I tell you, you are Peter and on this rock I will build my church and the Gates of Hell will not prevail against it!'

I allow myself to imagine that our little group is being asked the same question. We probably would have little difficulty in articulating what others, like the Gospel writers or Saint Paul, or the traditional doctrines, dogma and liturgies of the Church, say about who Jesus is. For some of us, it has been our life's calling to proclaim him. We feel happy enough to respond and at times almost clamour to do so. But when the question comes, as it does in unexpected moments – at times of personal or communal or global crisis, or extreme loneliness, or awareness of our growing physical frailty; wondering what our life's work has been all about, or our despair at the state of the world with its injustices, climate change, the greed of those with power and control, the fear and abnormality that has characterised the past few years – do the words hang in the air for a moment? 'Who do you say I am?' Is this followed by a pause? I know that, on a number of occasions in my life, I have paused, wondering how to answer. Jesus doesn't change the subject or move on. He waits, and I wait. You could say that I am waiting between Hades and the source of life. Of course, I know from somewhere deep within what my response will be; there can be no other than 'You are the Christ.'

But still I wait. How can I respond? How can I not respond? This is the question upon whose answer hinges the whole motivation for our spiritual journey. It is the question that comes at the beginning of our pilgrimage of faith and will be there at the end. Who do you say I am? Not what the others think – but you? It is something to which I will be called to respond not once but many times as I discover ever more deeply what it means to say, 'You are the Christ, the Son of the living God.' The journey of faith is always one of continuing revelation. For me, this question 'Who do you say I am?' is a constant companion, not in a threatening or stressful way but as a part of that mysterious friendship to which you, dear reader, and I, and all of humankind, are called. It has huge consequences in terms of how we share with others what we believe to be good news. It also influences how we regard our travelling companions on the journey of life and of faith.

I return to the present reality, to Caesarea Philippi. Suddenly I realise: the disciples knew this area. Despite their faith, they had their superstitions and they dreaded this place. It wasn't called the Gates of Hell for nothing. Jesus chose his stage perfectly. The drama was played out. The response was given and the journey continued, as does ours. We leave this place of contrasts and stark choices and I know that I am not the same as I was before coming here. As we drive away, I see rocks everywhere all around us. I realise that I am not asked to be a rock in or by myself but, along with countless others down through the ages, including you, the reader, to be the living stones out of which Jesus builds his Church.

Another day, another dawn; we move on. The sun blazes down from a cloudless sky. The Sea of Galilee is tranquil, sparkling, blue. We have already been on a boat trip that has gifted us with a glimpse of the eternal 'now' of presence. Out on the lake, we were there with Jesus and his disciples. Now we are on the shore at the water's edge. This is the spot where the risen Jesus did something as ordinary as preparing breakfast for his friends. This is the shore along which he and Peter strolled after they had eaten, when they had that healing, challenging conversation in which Peter was commissioned to 'feed the sheep'. This is the place from where, the evening before, they pushed out their boat, seven of them, to go fishing. They were somewhat in limbo at that time, unsure of what the future held. At Peter's instigation, they returned to the routine they had known before meeting Jesus. They went back to the familiar occupation of fishing. Not expecting anything out of the ordinary, they found themselves experiencing déjà vu. They caught nothing all night and then, with the encouragement of a stranger calling from the water's edge, they had a miraculous catch of fish. Who was this stranger? The eyes of love, those of the beloved disciple John, recognised him. But it was Peter who, impulsive as ever, jumped over the side of the boat and reached Jesus first.

We have come down to the water's edge. Knowing this account so well, it would be easy to miss some of the details that led to a healing of memory for Peter and the total assurance that he was accepted, forgiven and restored. All the details of this episode recalled significant events in Peter's pre-resurrection experience: the difficult night before, meeting with a stranger, the miraculous catch of fish, the recognition of who Jesus was, and the later adventure of getting out of the boat to cross the water and be with him. The charcoal fire lit on the beach perhaps gave Peter a flashback to the charcoal fire in the High Priest's courtyard where he had denied his Lord, and the breakfast called to mind the last supper Jesus served them, just as he was doing right now. In a sense, what was happening was a retelling of Peter's story, this time in the presence of the risen Lord. It was a time of redemptive remembering for Peter.

Jesus risen was the beginning of Peter's journey of restoration. What a transformation took place in this man, admittedly not overnight, but what a remarkable process of challenge, of stretching, of understanding, of encouragement, of appropriating the promises of God, all leading him to be, along with others, the sort of rock foundation upon which Jesus could build his Church.

After the redemptive remembering, Peter and Jesus go for a walk by the lakeside. And then comes the challenge, repeated three times: 'Simon, son of John, do you love me more than these others? Then feed my lambs, take care of my sheep.' It's as if each question invalidated each denial and, with each response from Peter, 'You know that I love you', he was appointed shepherd of the flock, a flock that did not belong to him but to Jesus who died for them and rose again that they might be liberated into the kingdom, with all that that implies of forgiveness, healing, hope, justice and, above all, love.

I am still at the water's edge, momentarily a little removed from the others. Impulsively, I take off my sandals and paddle in the refreshing water. I experience something as ordinary as sand between my toes. I am aware of the timelessness of this water and this sand, unchanged over thousands of years. Through this water Peter splashed his way to Jesus, sand between his toes, too. The same sun beams down, full of promise, resurrection and challenge. I remember that faithful old nomad Abraham to whom God gave the promise that he would make his descendants as numerous as the stars in the sky, or the sand on the seashore. The call to Abraham came just when he was thinking of settling down into retirement, on an ordinary night as he looked up at the stars in the night sky over Haran. The call to Peter came after something as ordinary as a fishing trip. The question for both was, in essence, the same: 'Do you love me?' Ordinary day turned into extraordinary moment.

As I reflect, I am conscious of several things. One centres not so much around who Jesus is, but who we are. When Abraham left home, letting go of many securities and the tribe where he was known and respected, embarking on a journey that others would have ridiculed, he was known as Abram, 'exalted father'. As he wandered from place to place, did he sometimes long for the security and seniority that gave him kudos and importance back in Haran? But there came a point, after much travelling and many tests of his love and faithfulness, when God sealed his covenant promise with him and gave him the new name of Abraham, meaning 'father of a multitude of nations'. This didn't mean that Abraham changed overnight into someone different. He would always have within him both Abram and Abraham. Both were part of who he was. His long journey of growing faithfulness and revelation as to who God is means that centuries later he is known in three major world religions, including Christianity, as our father in the faith.

There are many moments in Peter's life when his understanding of, and relationship with, God were stretched and challenged. In fact, this began with his very first intimate and personal encounter with Jesus when, after the miraculous catch of fish, he recognised his own unworthiness and effectively asked God to go away. Jesus' response was to tell him not to be afraid of non-familiarity and newness, but instead to come with him and learn as they travelled together. There followed many moments of recognition as Peter was released ever more deeply into an understanding of who Jesus is, as evidenced in his periodic outbursts of enthusiasm and faith. Actually, nearly all of the glimpses we have of Peter in the Gospels and the Acts of the Apostles record just such struggles and awakenings, one of the most dramatic being that at the Gates of Hell (which we had so recently visited), where Jesus gave him the name Peter. Thereafter in the Gospels he is often referred to as Simon Peter. For me, that encapsulates who Peter was and who he was becoming. He was surely and unmistakeably Simon, son of John, in all his broken humanity and his earthy human nature, but he was also Peter, who was in the long process of becoming, of being freed up, liberated more and more into who he really was.

Jesus knew the Simon in him as well as the Peter; he knew his human frailties, his particular Achilles heels. I think that is what Jesus meant when, on the night before his death at their last meal together, he used the old name, Simon. But beyond everything else, what sounds loud and clear throughout the whole Gospel story is Simon Peter's love for Jesus. So it is with me. At some stage, Jesus touched my life and I began a journey that will last the rest of my days. Sometimes I stay on the road and sometimes I wander off. It is, perhaps, the story of each one of us. We teeter between what some call our smaller self and our real self, but there comes a point, probably several points, when we know that there is no going back. We have made our declaration about who Jesus is for us and for this world. Jesus, in essence, gives us a new name, a new vision, a new purpose. I would venture to guess that the bottom line for us, as it was for Simon Peter, is simply that we love Jesus. 'You love him,' says Peter in one of his letters, 'even though you have never seen him. Though you do not see him, you trust him, and even now you are happy with a glorious, inexpressible joy' (1 Pt 1:8).

I am conscious, too, that there must be times, especially for people in the upper age bracket among whom I am now numbered, when we feel as if every day is ordinary, especially when comparing these days with how we have lived our lives, our vocations, when we were more physically active. We all have stories to tell of lives lived at the cutting edge, both in Ireland and in different parts of the world. Many of you, dear reader, will have had life experiences that have powerfully nurtured and shaped you into who you are today. But with the rate of change so accelerated nowadays, you can find yourselves in a world changed almost beyond recognition and filled with people too busy (that is, until the COVID-19 pandemic hit) to find out who you are or to listen to your stories. That lack of curiosity, interest or affirmation can lead to acute loneliness. Trapped in the ordinary, it would be so easy to believe that moments of recognition, fresh revelations of who Jesus is for you, are over. Not so.

Let us return to the lakeshore. Unseen presence is tangibly all around. I don my sandals once more. It is time to move on. I look down and see the grains of sand still clinging to my feet and between my toes. I, too, am part of the promise. I rejoin the group but, as I go through the ordinary motions of boarding the coach, what seems real is not the good-natured chatter around me but the words, wafted up from the water's edge, 'Do you love me?' Ordinary day turned into extraordinary moment. 'Lord, you know everything; you know I love you.'

At this stage of your journey,
who is Jesus for you?

What difference does your answer make to you;
what difference does it make to others?

A PRAYER

Thank you, Lord, for because of who you are, we
can come to know who we really are – beloved
daughters and sons of God.

Thank you, too, for promise, hope and fulfilment,
and for the restoration of relationship, which are
all part of the love
story between you and humankind.
Thank you for my being part of that story. Amen.

CHAPTER THREE

CONTRASTS

Mount Carmel; Ein Karem

*(1 Kings 18:20–46; Luke
1:39–80; John 1:6–34)*

SURREXIT ELIAS PROPHETA QUASI IGNIS ET VERBUM IPSIUS QUASI
facula ardebat ('Then there arose the fiery prophet Elijah
whose words blazed like a torch'). These words from
Ecclestiasticus, Chapter 48 are carved on the plinth of
an imposing statue of Elijah, which is the first thing
that arrests my attention as we approach the Carmelite
monastery and church of the Muhraqa on Mount Carmel.
Elijah has one foot on the neck of an unfortunate priest of
Baal (the cult of a male fertility god that was widespread
in ancient Phoenician and Canaanite lands) while his
right arm is raised, sword at the ready to strike. The statue
and its message provide quite a contrast to the peace of
this beautiful 'Garden of God' (which is what the name
Carmel means). But in Elijah's day, this mountain was
the main focus for Baal worship and it was here that he
confronted the prophets of Baal who were loyal to Queen
Jezebel, wife of Ahab, King of Israel. The challenge to the
onlookers was 'If the Lord is God, follow him! But if Baal

is God, then follow him.' The outcome is well known; the prophets of Baal were routed and Yahweh, God of Israel, vindicated; again a contrast, this one between pagan priests who had no success in setting fire to the wood of the offering and Elijah who called on God with unmistakeable results. The people responded, 'The Lord is God!'

As I climb to the platform that provides a viewing point from the monastery, and see stretching away into the distance the Jezreel Valley, the Kishon River, and even the Mediterranean Sea, I am reminded of another contrast, this time within Elijah himself. After the cataclysmic confrontation, Elijah, the fiery, seemingly fearless, prophet of God, was terrified and fled for his life. Standing on this platform gives me some idea of the vast distance he must have covered. Queen Jezebel had sworn to have him killed. He travelled almost two hundred miles and hid in a cave. God did not offer sympathy but instead, in a gentle whisper, a further challenge to return to the place whence he had fled, for there he would find many who were still faithful and who had not bowed the knee to Baal.

This is the only place we visit that relates exclusively to a character from the Old Testament, but what a character! It is impossible to ignore Elijah, the greatest prophet. I realise that some of my fellow pilgrims have difficulty with it, but I love the Old Testament. It is the cradle of the New Testament and provides such a colourful and vibrant backdrop to the unfolding love story of God's dealings with humankind. Perhaps I would have preferred to have been met by a sculpture of Elijah slumped under the broom tree, overcome with weariness and hopelessness, being ministered to by angels, or cowering in the cave, hiding from his pursuers as he waits for direction from God. With either of these Elijahs, I could empathise more. However, I know I have to take on board the reality of who Elijah really is – a person of contrasts, like all of us. The image of the fervent, indomitable prophet, a solitary figure standing for God against all the mighty pagan forces of Jezebel and Ahab, and the frightened, despairing, complaining fugitive who feels he is the only one left standing for righteousness, for the one God: both of these images are true. Together they sum up the man Elijah. This awareness does not diminish his stature but rather makes him appear more human and, therefore, more real. Broken and flawed yet strong and powerful; full of self-doubt and self-pity yet chosen, called and beloved; this is the paradox of Elijah and, perhaps, of every person.

Such awareness alerts me, not for the first time, to the danger of placing any human being on a pedestal. When we give in to such a subtle temptation, seeing only one facet of who they are, believing it to be the whole story, we are robbing them of their full humanity, placing them beyond the reach of 'ordinary' humankind, awarding them virtues and talents that they might never have claimed for themselves. There is an added danger that they may begin to assume the persona that others have created for them and believe that this is who they really are. Then, when they topple, as they almost inevitably will, their fall is all the greater and so much that has been attributed to them lies in ruins, including their very real and positive contributions to the world. Thank God that Elijah, after having so recently experienced both stunning victory and the bitter taste of fear, flight and seeming abandonment, was recalled to his real self. God was readily recognisable to Elijah in his powerful conquest of the priests of Baal. He was briefly euphoric as he proclaimed who God was and, perhaps, felt some vindication himself. After all, he was on the winning side!

But this was soon replaced by panic, depression and despair when Jezebel threatened him with just twenty-four hours to live. God was not so immediately recognisable to Elijah as he ran for his life. Hiding in the cave, he expected to find God in dramatic manifestations of earthquakes, wind or fire, as at Mount Carmel. But God was not in any of these. Instead, in something Elijah could so easily have missed or overlooked, he became aware of a faint sound borne on the breath of the wind, like a gentle whisper. In the encounter that followed, Elijah was recalled to his true self and to the essence of his vocation. He was reminded that he was not on his own, that he was not the only one who had sought to remain faithful. He was challenged to go back to the former scene of action to complete certain tasks, including anointing his successor. 'Mighty prophet, defender of the faith; terrified fugitive, almost suicidal' – all these and more formed part of the complex mix that seemingly defined Elijah. But this was not the last word. Elijah's true identity was, as it always had been, as a child of God, broken and beloved, called and chosen.

As we prepare to leave this place, I realise that I, too, am a person of contrasts. I know that often all that people see of me is the public persona; someone who seems confident enough, coping enough, faithful enough, joyful enough, loving enough, peaceful enough. But behind all this, there is also the other; the one who is vulnerable, fearful, insecure, longing for acceptance, questioning, at times despairing. Who am I – this, or the other? In the end, both are true, held together by the gentle whisper of a God who claims me in love and to whom I gladly yield.

We leave Mount Carmel but the questions it has raised don't quite leave me. In fact, I am reminded of them again in another encounter on another day. The little phrase 'the hill country of Judea' has always fascinated me, and today we are driving through these same hills to Ein Karem, the birthplace of John the Baptist. I relive some of the unforgettable events that occurred in this small, almost forgotten place. Mary journeyed through these hills, eager to visit her elderly cousin Elizabeth who was pregnant. What was she feeling as she made her way? Would Elizabeth understand the momentous event that had happened to her? Did she have some apprehension about her reception as she drew near the village? What would Elizabeth's husband, Zechariah, think? She needn't have worried. Zechariah had been struck dumb since the angelic visitation in the Temple and, when Mary came into view that day, the baby in Elizabeth's womb leapt with the joy of recognition.

We have been warned that our visit here will be quick, so we hurriedly leave the coach. We are not going to have the time to visit some of the sites. However, I pause for a moment to focus on the boy born to Elizabeth and Zechariah – right here in Ein Karem! Of course, this is not the beginning of God's love story with humankind, but it is probably the beginning of the most important chapter; I am so excited to be here, albeit briefly. Much more time would be needed to absorb the fact that this is where the great preparer of the Way was born. His name was John, which means the grace and mercy of God. This was what John the Baptist would give his life to proclaiming. This was someone who knew, even before his birth, the path he was destined to follow. Here he was a child, playing in the surrounding hills; here he grew to manhood, possibly exchanging frequent visits with his cousin from Nazareth; from here he left for the Judean wilderness, in all likelihood spending some time with the religious sect known as the Essenes. Around the age of thirty, after his godly upbringing and embrace of an ascetic lifestyle, John went public in the Judean Desert, fulfilling the prophecy his father made at his birth.

John's message was compelling, not only because he was shouting it, but because of his own authenticity and integrity. The people who flocked to hear him asked, 'What should we do?' He didn't give them a vague, pious or other-worldly answer, but rather one that was specific and relevant to every age, including our own. The people should prove by how they lived that they were making a fresh start. Those who had food and clothing should share with those who had not. Tax collectors needed to be honest in their dealings. Soldiers should be upright and trustworthy. My thoughts shift to the first chapter of John's Gospel where I sense the true mettle of this amazing man. Here he is portrayed as the proclaimer and forerunner of the Messiah. Our attention is focussed not so much on him as on the one whom he has come to announce: 'God sent John the Baptist to tell everyone about the light so that everyone might believe because of his testimony. John himself was not the light; he was only a witness to the light. The one who was the true light, who gives light to everyone was going to come into the world.'

John's ministry became so well known that he aroused the interest of the powers that be. The Jewish leaders sent priests and Temple assistants from Jerusalem to quiz him. 'Who are you?' they asked. 'Are you the Messiah? Are you Elijah?' And I recall that many people believed that John was Elijah come back to life, based on Malachi's prophecy, 'Look, I am sending you the prophet Elijah before the great and dreadful day of the Lord arrives' (Mal 4:5). John refuted any claim to be anyone other than who he knew himself to be, namely a voice in the wilderness urging his hearers to prepare a straight pathway for the Lord's coming. He had a clear sense of where he came from and who he was – son, certainly, of Elizabeth and Zechariah, but also the last of the prophets of the old dispensation. He was clearly part of that long history of those messengers of God, like Elijah, who fearlessly proclaimed the Word of the Lord. He had no axe to grind. His rootedness gave him humility, a true sign of greatness. There were many occasions during his brief public ministry when he could have claimed power and status for himself but he resolutely turned his face from what he knew did not belong to him.

Sometimes on this pilgrimage it can seem as if we are trying to pack too much in, and yet I don't want to miss anything. It's just that John the Baptist has always fascinated me and I would like more time here to ponder. There is one incident in particular that I recall with awe. When those sent to question him persisted, he eventually said something that sets my spirit on tiptoe with anticipation: 'Among you is standing he whom you don't know. He will soon begin his ministry.' Right here in the crowd is the one you have been waiting for and you don't know him; you can't recognise him! And I am not worthy to even untie his sandals. (In other words, 'I am not worthy even to be his slave.') The very next day he saw

Jesus coming towards him and said, 'There is the Lamb of God who takes away the sin of the world.' In so doing he became the template for all those preparers of the Way who would follow him down through the centuries to the present day and on into the future – priests, pastors, teachers, prophets; those (including – and this is the mind-blowing bit – me!) whose task is always to point beyond themselves to the one who comes.

John knew how to let go, to climb down, to say yes in the darkness to the purposes of God. When some of his disciples left to follow Jesus, he released them with a spirit that rejoiced because the 'bridegroom was near' even though, in his humanity, there must have been an increasing sense of loneliness. He began life in the darkness of the womb, here in Ein Karem. He ended his life in the darkness of Herod Antipas' dungeons. The first was a prison of love that was filled with joy and opened out into life. But when power, control and fear were cornered by his courageous witness, he was arrested, imprisoned and ultimately beheaded. Can you imagine the sense of loss for someone who had lived out in the open, never again to see the blue of the sky or feel the warmth of the sun on his face? In the darkness of his prison cell, did he look up and remember this very hill country, the beauty that had enriched his childhood, the freedom of his early years? Of course, in his humanity, he would have had doubts and fears and questions, maybe even wondering if he had got it all wrong, if he had failed to hear God aright, if what he had given his life to, for which he had risked everything, had been only a figment of his imagination. And if that was so, who was he – and who was Jesus? There is a poignant moment when John voiced his doubts. He got a message to his disciples to ask Jesus the question that had now become so big for him that he doubts both his own and Jesus' identity, that of which he had once been so sure. 'Are you the Messiah we've been expecting, or should we keep looking for someone else?' (Lk 7:18–20)

I've always been glad of Jesus' response; not 'Yes, I am' but 'Go back to John and tell him what you have seen and heard – the blind see, the lame walk, the lepers are cured, the deaf hear, the dead are raised to life and the Good News is being preached to the poor' (Lk 7:22). Jesus used words of the prophet Isaiah to confirm for John the signs of the kingdom. Then he slipped into the message that is one of the hidden Beatitudes of the Gospels, 'God blesses those who are not offended by me' (Lk 7:23). I think what he is saying is, 'You are blessed, John. Don't doubt now. What you have witnessed to so faithfully is true.' Jesus loved his cousin John; he once said of him, 'Of all who have ever lived none is greater than John.' But then he added something that used to puzzle me greatly: 'Yet even the most insignificant person in the Kingdom of God is greater than he is' (Lk 7:28). As time has passed, I have realised that Jesus is not saying anything negative about John but rather that John was the last and greatest of the prophetic voices before Jesus and, that from this point onwards, everyone who ever lived would have the opportunity to recognise and appropriate that mutuality of belovedness that betokens the kingdom of heaven within. John stood outside this mystery but was still able to rejoice. He challenges me to prepare a way within myself so that again and again I may welcome the one who comes. He calls me to let go, to climb down, to decrease and, perhaps, to rediscover my vocation, to open myself up to a relationship of love. In so doing, I discover who I really am.

Before we take our leave of Ein Karem, I pause to silently salute this fearless prophetic voice who walks the path of descent and points us beyond himself to the Lamb of God. As we board the coach, I am jolted by another moment of recognition. I suddenly remember that this very hill country of Judea was the first to hear the two best-known and best-loved songs of praise, cherished by Christians around the world and down through the centuries. They are, of course, the words sung by Mary after Elizabeth's greeting and those sung by Zechariah at the birth of his little son. As we drive back to Jerusalem, this hill country of Judea resounds for me with an outpouring of the Magnificat for the one who is the Way and with the Benedictus for the one who was the preparer of the Way. In a moment of gratitude and awareness, my soul, too, 'glorifies the Lord' who gives 'light to those in darkness and guides our feet into the way of peace'. Despite the shortness of the visit, what a day we have had!

Who do you think you are?

Can you spend some time today
with the Benedictus?

A PRAYER

Lord, life is full of contrasts and choices.
Sometimes they bewilder and confuse me and
I don't know which way to turn. In such times,
and in all times, help me to trust you.
Amen.

CHAPTER FOUR

HANDMAID OF
THE LORD

Nazareth

(Luke 1:26–38)

SOMETIMES ON THIS PILGRIMAGE, I HAVE TO REMIND myself that I am actually here, in Israel. The places, the names, the sayings of local people, are indelibly printed on my mind and have been all my life, but to actually be in a place that, on one level, is so familiar to me and, on another, that I don't know at all, is a strange experience. This is certainly true of today's excursion: I am excited, for today we are going to Nazareth. I wonder, as I look around the coach at my fellow travellers, are they feeling the same? This is where we first encounter Mary, the person I approach with more wonder and awe than any other figure in Scripture (with the exception of Jesus himself). At the same time, I know that if she is to be an inspiration and encouragement to all of us, we need to see her as being fully human, someone who wrestled with the same problems and hopes as we do, someone who broke through to a whole new awareness of what believing is all about, someone who understood more than most the why of the Incarnation – yet even she did not fully understand. She accepted mystery as part of the journey and learned through struggle, not through passive submission, what trust and surrender signify. For me, Mary is a model of what it means to be a follower of Jesus, not because she portrays some sort of idealised perfection far removed from the realities of what we have to live, but because she is fully human. In her humanity, she inspires me to believe that it is possible to choose the road less travelled, to believe in the power of one person to bring about change, to trust that our lives can make a difference, often far greater than we would ever dare to imagine as we wrestle to reach the point of saying yes to co-operating with God in his loving purpose for the world.

'Can any good thing come out of Nazareth?' This was the question posed by Nathaniel in the first chapter of John's Gospel (Jn 1:46). I have to confess, as we enter the town, that those words are echoing in my mind. Modern Nazareth is noisy and bustling and has nothing very distinctive about it. But then our coach takes us to the huge Basilica of the Annunciation. Our group momentarily scatters to wander around this beautiful building, so cool and spacious inside. There is even an area where it is 'agreed' that the angel Gabriel met Mary with the incredible news that she would have a son who would be 'the Son of the Most High God'. There are stained-glass windows and sculptures, artworks of many kinds

– but something is missing. Something is not 'doing it' for me. It seems too grand and somehow remote from the Mary of the Gospels who inspires me and gives me courage and hope. I have never been a great admirer of many of the statues of Mary for that very reason. They portray an idealised perfection far removed from the harsh realities of life that we are called to live. So I admit to a little disappointment. I don't feel connected.

And then – I find her. I find the Mary who stands between the living and the dead, the Mary who waits in the gap between ordinariness and mystery, the Mary who stands on tiptoe between the old and the new, the Mary who, because of her quiet faithfulness, moves beyond the acceptable cultural and religious norms of her day, the Mary of courage, the Mary who chooses, the Mary who has already experienced an inner nativity in terms of knowing who she is in God. In the lower church, in an alcove near a door, is a statue that makes up for all the others I have seen. There is no one else around. I have a blessed moment on my own simply to be with Mary, my sister! Here is a young girl, hair loose, striding forward as if to meet the future and all that it may hold, her face eager and alight, embodying the 'yes' that is given after the questions, the wonder and awe, the struggle. Having waited on the threshold, she now steps over it, into an unknown future, leaving herself open to being impregnated by a love that changes and continues to transform the world. Love waits for her response. It's a holy pause. Gabriel waits; all heaven waits. Mary does not know what the living-out of that 'yes' will entail, but she gives herself to it willingly and with complete trust in God. 'I am the Lord's handmaiden. May it happen to me and through me as you have said.' The birth pangs had already begun, even before her physical pregnancy developed, even before the hard labour in the stable of Bethlehem. In fact, with her ongoing inner nativity, those birth pangs would continue throughout the rest of her life as she embraced God's will for her life, with joy and acute anguish. Sorrow like a sharp sword would pierce her heart when she allowed this eternal 'happening' to have existence, and as she thus became part of the longed-for transformation of all things.

I reflect that, at any decisive moment in our lives, at the point of heightened awareness where we know that we are in the presence of all that is holy, something other than ourselves tips us over into the flow of something more, something beyond us; but it is not that we are creatures of a blind fate. The Great Lover awaits the free response of the beloved, for love, the essence of God, never wins through by force. It is a drawing, a wooing. True trust and surrender do not come by repressing questions, doubts and fears but by being present to them, voicing them, facing the reality of what such a response will involve and then 'letting it be done'. So it was with Mary. Behind Mary stand Ruth, Esther, Rizpah and countless others, each faced with a hard choice, though none as hard as hers. Each one is called 'for such a time as this' to wrestle with God, challenged to act for the deliverance of the people, for restoration of right relationships. Mary, this young woman called to incarnate 'Thus says the Lord' in such a unique way, is commissioned to bear a truth that will not be understood or accepted by the majority of those in her faith community – such a lonely position to be in. Eyes wide open in the Spirit, willing to cast her lot in with mystery, her *fiat*, her readiness to accept God's will, comes at last. I am so grateful that this process is recorded for us by Luke, a process that gives all those who are open to God and who wrestle with hard choices courage and hope.

Mary knew how to be present to presence. I realise that we have heard a lot about 'presence' over recent years, but thinking and talking is no substitute for practising. Mary dared to be open to what was unfolding before her and being open meant that she also allowed herself to be vulnerable. Just imagine accepting this scenario for what it was and taking Gabriel at face value – a heavenly messenger, mind-blowing enough in itself, but a heavenly messenger announcing something so preposterous and unbelievable as the Annunciation, and yet she was able to say, in the end, 'Let it be. Let it be done unto me. Let it be done unto me according to your word.' Mary recognised that infinite love could never be boxed in and confined and so she surrendered to mystery. Even at my age, I like to believe that an inner nativity is still taking place within me. That inner nativity, that dawning awareness, those glimpses of something more, I have to allow happen to me. That is where the letting go, the abandonment, comes in. I can take heart from Mary, who did not allow the extreme ordinariness and drudgery of her life to define who she was, and who allowed its grip on her life to loosen so that she was able to let go and say, 'Let it be.'

As I continue to gaze at this wonderful sculpture, I come to the conclusion that the artist had a particular image of Mary in mind. I am sure that one of the influences on the work was the image of Mary hastening across the hill country of Judea to visit her cousin Elizabeth. Through Elizabeth, Mary had her encounter and commission confirmed by a visible sign and, from a place of awe and wonder, from the depths of her being, came the song. She discovered her voice in a whole new way and sang out, for all people and for all time, a song of liberation, salvation and freedom that would be actually incarnated in her by the power of the Holy Spirit. It is the climax of all the songs sung throughout the centuries, those of her forebears Miriam, Deborah and Hannah, all of whom sang songs of salvation but were not allowed to see what Mary had been given to see, or to hear what Mary had been given to hear. This is the song of a prophet who knew herself blessed because of what had been revealed to her, who knew she had to sing it out with every part of her body, soul and spirit. The song gathers into the eternal now of God all that has passed and all that is yet to be, and declares the overriding faithfulness of God to all those who know their need of him and his ever-present mercy, his steadfast love. My mind leaps forward about thirty-three years and I have a sudden moment of awareness. I have a strong sense that Mary, even in the midst of her unspeakable anguish, was singing the Magnificat again at Calvary. In fact, it had probably been woven into the very fabric of her life ever since her first encounter with mystery; with Gabriel. This was part of her continuing surrender. Just after the Annunciation, she sang out to bring into being that which God had purposed through her. At the cross, I like to think the song was heard again, and with it came transformation.

In this moment, in front of this statue, Mary is fully present to me. The God of surprises, God who is so often the god of the unexpected, has reassured me that he delights to work through the little, the humble, the unknown. All that he requires of me is my *fiat*, my 'yes'. I think back over my life to times I have been faced with significant choices, times when I have prevaricated as well as times when I have simply seized the moment, believing that God was in it and that he is faithful and trustworthy. I pause and think again. Those 'kairos moments' – special times – were not really choices but rather giftings of acute awareness where there was only one response I could make, a response that would make me a tiny part of God's action plan for the world. Mary reminds me that she, along with countless others throughout the centuries, including myself, are simply and amazingly 'handmaids of the Lord'. I can move away from this encounter feeling that, in spending time with what is, for me, a unique image, I have met with her who is blessed among women.

I look around for the rest of my party and find them gathering at a spot believed to be the site of the house where Mary lived that had a well close by. Tradition tells us that the angel Gabriel appears to Mary as she draws water from a well, an ordinary, essential task that she must have undertaken at least once, probably several times, each day. This makes perfect sense to me. Wells in the ancient world, and still in many countries today, are natural meeting places. Water is essential to life. Without it, none of us can function. It is usually women or children who are sent to draw the water required for both family and livestock. Even in countries like our own, Ireland, there are hundreds of wells, most of them no longer in normal use but regarded as holy because they are reputed to be places of blessing, of cures, of new life. For many, they have become focal points for pilgrimage, just as we are pilgrims in Nazareth today.

So although Gabriel's meeting with Mary at a well is not found in Scripture, I have no problem in accepting the tradition that this is what happened. I reflect on how many encounters are recorded of significant meetings at wells, most of them involving women. When Hagar, slave girl of Sarah, runs away from her mistress, she encounters an angel of the Lord at a well or desert spring. Thereafter the name given to it is 'the Well of the Living One who sees me'. It is at a well that Abraham's servant, in search for a wife for Isaac, meets Rebekah, and at a well that Jacob encounters Rachel, the love of his life. Moses, fleeing from Egypt, meets his wife-to-be, Zipporah, at a well. The best-known recorded encounter in Scripture is that of Jesus with the Samaritan woman when she comes to Jacob's well to draw water. This is the first time in John's Gospel that Jesus reveals his true identity to anyone – and he does so to an outsider, to someone whom others despise (for being a Samaritan), and to a woman! The implications of this meeting are huge and perhaps many of them still have relevance today.

I bring myself back to focussing on Mary. Whether this particular place is the actual spot where this moment of destiny occurred is not as important to me as what it symbolises – that unequivocal response from a young woman of faith to a calling that will change the world forever. The words that flood into my mind come from childhood, words we knew by heart, 'Behold the handmaid of the Lord.' There are now many new and different translations but the word 'behold' sticks with me. It is more than simply looking or casually seeing. It is an exhortation to really see, perhaps not only with our physical sight but with our minds and our hearts as well. It means arriving at that point of recognition in our spiritual seeing that gives us that 'aha' moment, that grasping at mystery that, paradoxically, can never actually be fully grasped. 'Behold' is an old word, a beautiful word. It's not used so much today but I really don't think any word can replace it. If you break the word down, there is a sense in which, for me, it means to hold something to be, to be true, or even to hold the person or event 'into being', into existence. In her response at the Annunciation, Mary became ever more fully the handmaid of the Lord. As she let it be 'done unto her' as God desired, she could declare who she was and who she was becoming. In the months – and years – that followed, she continued to hold into being that which was promised.

To truly behold can lead us to unfamiliar places, to different ways of seeing, to uncomfortable insights, to risking the loss of some relationships and things we have held dear. It can challenge our comfort zones, disturb our peace, widen our horizons and sometimes take us where we don't want to go. Anyone can behold. It doesn't take a special education or a particular position in society, or a list of achievements and successes. All it requires is a heart sufficiently humble and open to being surprised and to receiving. As I dare, however stumblingly, to let it be done to me according to God's loving purpose, I know that I discover a little bit more of who I am; I recognise more clearly the calling and know myself, too, to be a handmaid of the Lord.

But our group tells me that it is time to go. As I leave, I picture again the young Mary with her water jar, her attention arrested by this totally unexpected, divine encounter that asks everything from her, this encounter whose outcome will transform the world. In this moment she does not know that the son she will bear will be, in himself, a well, a holy spring from whom those who are thirsting for life in its fullness, for right relationships, can draw an unending supply. In this moment she does not hear the words, 'Let anyone who is thirsty come to me and drink!' In this moment she does not see a cross or hear the tortured cry, 'I thirst.' But in this moment, and for all eternity, she says 'Yes', as Jesus, too, will say 'Yes', and through such responses the water of life flows for all the world. I am so glad that we came to Nazareth!

'I am the Lord's servant. Let it be done to me as you have said.' What would it mean for you to make such a declaration?

Can you make the Magnificat your own song of praise? Which line speaks to you?

A PRAYER

Thank you, Lord, for your love that invites but does not coerce. And also for the times when you have 'tipped me over' into life, thank you.

Lord, the whole of humankind is thirsty, thirsty for love, for belonging, for identity, for meaning. May they find in you the well of living water. Amen.

CHAPTER FIVE

CROSSING
OVER

Sea of Galilee; Bethlehem

(*Ecclesiastes 3:1–15*)

WE HAVE COME TO TIBERIAS. THERE ARE MANY PLACES that I want to see in this part of the Holy Land, chief among them being a boat trip on the Sea of Galilee. I can see that my companions share my sense of expectancy. It is early morning. So much of Jesus' ministry occurred around this shoreline or out on the water itself. If I look to one side of the lake, to Galilee, I see the buildings of Tiberias and other smaller settlements, a mix of ancient and modern, bustling with ordinary, everyday activity. If I look to the other side, I see hills and space and mystery; the unknown. This side is known in Scripture as the Decapolis (meaning ten towns), which were Greek (Gentile) settlements, an uncomfortable area for Jewish people like the disciples who believed that the inhabitants of the Decapolis were pagans and not to be associated with unless absolutely necessary. Other boats are out on the lake now, taking advantage of the stillness and relative coolness before the sun climbs high in the sky and the crowds multiply. In this moment, as I look towards the 'mystery' side, I sense that this is how it was when Jesus said to his disciples, 'Let's cross over to the other side.' They left the crowds behind and other boats followed them. There was the sudden fierce storm and the accompanying terror of the disciples, who believed that their last hour had come, especially as Jesus was asleep in the stern, seemingly oblivious to the imminent danger and his friends' distress. In their panic, they forgot who it was that was in the boat with them, or perhaps they didn't really yet know. They accused him of not caring. Their journey with Jesus, as is ours, was one of dawning revelation as their eyes were gradually opened to who this person really was. There was always more for them, as there is for us, to discover about this Jesus whom even the winds and waves obey.

The phrase 'the other side' is common parlance today and it is one that evokes fear in many. It signifies unknown territory, be it an actual physical place, or people who differ from us in their culture, language, belief systems, traditions, religion, race or gender identity. In the North of Ireland, right throughout our thirty-year conflict and now into twenty-four years of the peace process, 'the other side' still tends to dominate, with all its underlying drumbeats of fear. Looking back, we can recognise and give thanks for those of good courage who reached out and built bridges of understanding, who crossed over because they knew our lives as a healthy community depended upon a shared future, who braved the storms of aggression and bitterness, who felt the fear and did it anyway. In spite of all those efforts, we are not quite there yet. But think of where we would be if so many had not got into the boat, showing that good courage which God honours. However, in the last few years I have the sense that all this has been but the preface, the training ground for something else, something that will require in large measure that courage that comes from knowing deep within our spirits that the final outcome belongs to the God who has already overcome. And it is not that, in seeking to journey, we will not be afraid. We will encounter fear as we embrace the future but we can persist because Jesus has already faced the worst fear and darkness and has come through. That being so, when the challenge comes to once again cross over to the other side, whatever that may signify, it will be possible for us to walk his way.

Although the water was beautifully calm on our boat trip, our guide told us that storms could spring up on the lake with practically no warning. At the time of writing, January 2022, I look back, not, this time, to 2018 and our pilgrimage, but to March 2020. None of us could have imagined the storm that was about to break upon us in the form of the coronavirus pandemic. We were busy in our own 'Tiberias', going about our ordinary lives, rushing from this to that, with no time to be, or even to reflect on, the 'something more', the unseen world all about us, on the meaning of life and faith and love. I'm not saying that the ordinary is bad; in fact, it is the very stuff of our lives and most of it is good, but it is not the totality of who we are. Unless challenged and burdened by the crises and traumas of life such as serious illness, loss of employment, grief at the death of someone we love, or the frailty and isolation that often accompanies old age, we continued as normal, whatever 'normal' is. We had little time, or maybe little inclination, to 'cross over to the other side', that is, to step past the familiar into the unknown world of new ideas, fresh understanding of what it means to be part of humankind, letting go of some of the convictions that we clutched so tightly to ourselves (those things that, to us, seem to sum up our entire identity) in order to leave space for the vast and as yet unexplored territory of God's continuous creative love and boundless mercy. By and large, we were content to go through the motions of our particular faith practice without thinking, or without daring to abandon ourselves even a little to the mystery of deeper relationship with the God we know as yet only partially. Our lives were drowning out the whispered invitation to something more, to join the dance of the beloved community that is God – Father, Son and Holy Spirit.

And then there came the sudden storm of the pandemic, terrifying, threatening, and all-pervasive. At least the disciples had prior knowledge of the storms that could break upon the Sea of Galilee without warning. Most of us had no prior experience of this storm of pandemic that is still menacing the world and has left such devastation in its wake, a silent, insidious enemy striking without fear or favour, causing acute anxiety, untold anguish, lamentation and grief. Our children have been robbed of crucial experiences of learning and growing, not only of formal education but of social development, and of experiencing all the joys of living and of youth. There has been devastation due to loss of jobs and livelihoods, threatened economic collapse, fragile mental health due to isolation and seeming lack of purpose, and extreme loneliness, especially for those shielding and elderly people living alone. There are also the numerous partially hidden people suffering from undiagnosed symptoms with fear and dread, and those who are diagnosed with coronavirus or other illnesses but unable to get the treatment they need because the tidal wave of pandemic has swamped all available resources. Even with the reality of a coronavirus vaccine, fear still nibbles at the edge of our consciousness as we wonder about the new variants. Accompanying this tempest of emotions is an acute awareness of millions of our sisters and brothers in the poorer, forgotten parts of the planet who have yet to receive the help that we so readily claim as our right. In our terror, our helplessness and, yes, our anger, we have shouted out to a God who has seemed to be asleep, 'Do you not care that we are drowning?' Where are you, God, in all of this? And I have realised, yet again, how fragile a thing is trust; it is so easily shattered. But it has also come to me, not for the first time in my life, that the real meaning of faithfulness is not so much that I cling on to God but that he is clinging on to me and will never let me go.

I reflect on other things as well. For example, I recognise how often I have heard the invitation to cross over, to reach out to someone who is different, to embrace a new idea or a concept of inclusion that initially seems a step too far, to launch out into new territory that may take me to a place where I don't feel comfortable. I think again of the storms that have raged either because others have disagreed with the 'crossing' I have taken or because my own trust has flickered and wavered. I remember the times when Jesus seemed to be asleep and I felt I was drowning in waves of misunderstanding, loneliness and fear. I think of how 'the other side' within me can also be frightening; what is often called my 'true self' or my 'bigger self'. I know that I am more comfortable with my more familiar, lesser, or smaller, self. Yet I also know that the invitation from Jesus is 'Let's cross over.' That will involve a letting go, not once but many times, of what I have felt has shaped my identity, or even determined who I am. I am afraid of the unknown, of the unexplored territory within. I can so easily forget that I am not alone, that Jesus is also in the boat that is me.

Sometimes it is not until the storm hits and our spirits cry out in fear or despair that we sense the beginning of a great calm and we know, even if we're not fully there yet, that we have advanced a little further in trust and abandonment and can, in wonder, give thanks for the glimpses of more that lies waiting for us within. Right now we stand on the threshold of something new. We may feel that we can do very little at the moment, but we can still 'cross over' right where we are. We can commit in our inner beings to crossing over in our thoughts, attitudes, prayers and limited actions, crossing over from hatred to love, from injury to pardon, from doubt to faith, from despair to hope.

I am back on the Sea of Galilee. The water laps against the side of the boat. I feel myself overtaken by a sense of presence. From somewhere deep within me I hear the words 'Peace, be still.' Who is speaking? I realise in an 'eternity moment', a moment that is timeless, that Jesus has never abandoned the boat that is me, the true me. I reach towards the mystery and commit myself again to crossing over. Dear reader, whatever the storm, Jesus has never, ever abandoned the boat that is you. May you wait patiently for the Lord. And may you, too, be overtaken this day by a sense of presence and hear the words 'Peace, be still.'

Peace is in short supply in many places on earth. And now we are no longer in Tiberias. We have arrived at Bethlehem, birthplace of Jesus, the Prince of Peace. From my window in the Manger Square Hotel I see, outlined against the sky, a minaret; I hear the call to prayer – *Allahu Akbar* (God is great). It is Ramadan and I know that we are on the cusp of the holiest day in the Islamic year, marking the moment when the Qur'an was revealed to Mohammed. The town is crowded with pilgrims. It is my first time hearing the Muslim call to prayer in person. There is something haunting about it. For Christians, Bethlehem is the place that marks one of the holiest days in the Christian year, the birth of Jesus. Even now, in June, the town is crowded with Christian pilgrims. What memories and emotions the name Bethlehem evokes for me – I am excited and apprehensive at the same time. My overriding emotion is the desire to see the various sites that form the backdrop to the greatest story ever told. Perhaps it is my imagination, but I can sense a certain uneasiness in the streets outside our hotel. And I cannot forget the wall, the West Bank Barrier, erected to keep people out or in, depending on which 'side' they are from. I am no stranger to such things. There remain today, twenty-four years into the peace process, more than ninety 'peace walls', barriers or interfaces, in the city of Belfast. And we have come to Bethlehem (the name means 'the house of bread') to remember and pay homage to the one who called himself the Bread of Life, the one who incarnates inclusion, compassion, welcome, peace and, above all, love.

As I seek to let go of some of the mindset I have carried with me, like excess baggage, I reflect that the Bethlehem of today is not so very different from two thousand years ago. Bread is both ordinary and extraordinary; ordinary in that it is the stuff of everyday life; extraordinary in that, without it, i.e. without sustenance, we cannot live. Where God chooses to make his dwelling place is in the ordinariness of our everyday lives with all their joys and sorrows, anxieties and busyness. He lands bang into the middle of the conflict, the suspicion, the injustice, the dehumanisation and lack of compassion that characterise the world as we know it. He comes to us as an extraordinary gift, as the source – the bread – of life without which we cannot fully live. So where else could he have been born but in Bethlehem? A space probe travelling for many years through space and landing on a comet is as nothing compared with this, namely that God, creator of the universe, at a specific point in human history, becomes incarnate, landing on planet earth in Bethlehem, house of bread, to reveal to us that we and all of humankind are his beloved. In that sense, I imagine that the desire of our hearts is for a deeper 'Bethlehem experience'. But we cannot conjure that up. We cannot just make it happen. It is not reached by great deeds or mighty efforts or shows of strength. This is not the way God chooses to come to us, nor is it the way we are called by God to take. God very deliberately comes in hiddenness, in littleness, and in vulnerability. So, if we are in earnest, the way by which we come is also by the little road to Bethlehem. It is this place that God chooses as the birthplace for his Son, in littleness and obscurity. In his person he becomes the bridge where God meets us, and relationships with him and with each other are restored.

It's all about encounter and building relationships. It is the call to enter into friendship with the other, a relationship that becomes a source of life for both. And with the building of relationships, attitudes change. Something is resurrected, hope is restored, and a new understanding comes into play. This does not require great deeds, mighty efforts or shows of strength. It is simply to practise the sacrament of encounter, a path that is walked by countless people, all over the world, who live in relative hiddenness, in littleness and vulnerability. They know their calling is to simply be present and aware. Such unnamed saints are truly travelling that little road to Bethlehem, practising the sacrament of encounter. Their choice, as is mine, is essentially whether they are going to be a bridge or a wall.

Returning to the present day, one of the many things I love about Pope Francis is that he continually practises that sacrament of encounter. His papacy has been marked by nurturing relationships, with God, with others, and with the whole of creation. He not only seeks to build bridges; he is, in himself, a bridge. I was especially moved by his visit to Iraq in the spring of 2021 when he visited places sacred to Jews, Christians and Muslims. But it was his meeting with the ninety-year-old Grand Ayatollah Ali al-Sistani, Iraq's top Shiite cleric, that is stamped indelibly on my heart. Although the security was high, they met in al-Sistani's simple rented home and, for nearly an hour, shared together in humility and equality; truly a sacrament and a sign of hope for the world.

In his latest book, *Let Us Dream: The Path to a Better Future*, Pope Francis reminds us that God continually invites us to join with him as co-creators of the world, a world that is always being remade. We are called to be creators of our future. He challenges us to dare to seize the moment and to dream big. He says, 'We need a movement of people who we know need each other, who have a sense of responsibility to others and to the world. We need to proclaim that being kind, having faith and working for the common good are great life goals that need courage and vigour.'* This, for me, is about daring to live the future we long for in the present moment. It is about practising the sacrament of encounter. It is about seeking to be in, our very selves, a bridge. It is about walking that little road to Bethlehem, in company with the one who dared to dream so big that we have, to date, only skimmed the surface of what he has in his heart and mind for humankind.

I return to 2018 and our pilgrimage. It's time for me to join my fellow pilgrims for dinner. With the echoes of the call to prayer still ringing in my ears, I turn away from the window with a sudden surge of gratitude to the God who exquisitely planned this supreme explosion of love into time and space in such a hidden, little way – this open secret that continues to transform the world – and me! In this place of tension and uneasy peace, I give thanks that not only in Bethlehem and Belfast but in so many unexpected places there are people dismantling unseen walls and becoming bridges, flinging their affirmation of faith against whatever darkness would seek to engulf humankind, that life is stronger than death, that hope can emerge from places of despair, that from the anguished corners of the earth an alleluia of joy can yet be awakened, that the weak can confound the powerful and that love will triumph over hatred. I am now feeling more ready to visit the sites that must hold within their very stones something of the mystery and the glory of the Incarnation. Welcome to Bethlehem!

* Pope Francis with Austen Ivereigh, *Let Us Dream: The Path to a Better Future* (London: Simon & Schuster UK Ltd, 2020), p. 6.

What constitutes the 'other side' for you?

Are you being challenged to cross over?

What are the storms, imagined or real, that
might prevent you?

A PRAYER

Lord, it is sometimes hard and lonely to be a
bridge. When I feel like that, keep me aware of
the bigger picture.

And when storms hit, may I know your
presence, which is peace. Amen.

CHAPTER SIX

A SONG
OF HOPE

Bethlehem

(Luke 2:8–20; Micah 5:2–5)

ONE OF THE THINGS THAT I LOVE ABOUT THIS PILGRIMAGE
is that those who were always shadowy figures on the pages
of Scripture are now 'becoming', for me, real people, even
if there are few, if any, of their spoken words to be found in
Scripture. It is as if they have a voice beyond sound, a song
without words that resonates with hope even in the midst
of darkness and despair. We are still in Bethlehem where,
in one sense, it all began. Bethlehem, with its memories of
Christmas, initially conjures up for most of us images of
joy and comfort, memories of childhood when the whole
world seemed magic. In reality, we know that this is not so.
God's plan, born out of his unchanging, unconditional love
for the world, had been in his heart throughout aeons. That
plan entered recorded history with the towering figures of
Abraham, Isaac and Jacob, followed by Joseph and Moses
and countless other lawgivers and prophets and nameless
faithful ones (along with those who sought to stymie God's
plan due to their own rebellion, power-seeking and greed),

until the time was right and Mary appeared. Hers was the 'yes' that would open a door for the world that could never again be closed.

Advent, Lent and Easter are inextricably interlinked. Already, in the stable at Bethlehem, the shadow of the cross fell upon the manger. Joy and hope, pain and anguish, were woven together from the very beginning, combining to form a timeless song of hope, a melody both old and ever new. It tells of disturbing peace, outrageous hope and radical love. And it seems that the two elements that enable us to hear the melody, and sometimes even to join in the song, are the experiences of great love and great suffering. It may even be that any deep prayer (which is really our love relationship with God) is not possible without our willingness to embrace both these elements.

Our coach takes us next to the outskirts of modern Bethlehem. This is assumed to be close to Boaz's field, while nearby is a restaurant that bears the name of Ruth. I feel as if I have been here before. This area or little village is known as Beit Sahour, 'the village of the watching'. I have always wanted to visit the Shepherds' Field Chapel, so evocative of my favourite season of the year, Advent, the four-week period before Christmas, a time of watching and waiting. We enter the large cave below the chapel and find that we are the only group currently visiting this site. We know that this will change quickly, so while we have it to ourselves we find somewhere to sit down and listen to our spiritual accompanier. We are told that it would have been just such a place that the shepherds used for shelter while looking after their flocks in the countryside around Bethlehem. That part of the Christmas narrative beginning 'Now there were shepherds abiding in the fields, keeping watch over their flocks by night' is so well loved and so much part of the mystery of eternity breaking into time that we never tire of hearing it. We continue to be intrigued and fascinated by it, even after we've left the magic of childhood behind. When we hear the familiar words, we are, in a timeless moment, transported back to that night when the heavens blazed with stars and the night was filled with a song of hope that reverberates down the centuries and awakens hardened hearts or minds imprisoned by scepticism to the thought that maybe, just maybe, it actually happened. Maybe, just maybe, this world is more than we know. Maybe, just maybe, in a spiritual dimension there are armies of heaven's angels under the command of a God whose nature is always love.

Before the next coachload of pilgrims arrives, there is a little time for quiet reflection. I think of the shepherds. They were at the margins of society, hardly noticed by those who mattered in the world of their day. But woven into the very fabric of their everyday, humdrum lives was the admonition to keep watch. It is thought that these shepherds were hired to look after sheep that would be used as sacrifices in the Temple worship. Their livelihood, the safety of their flocks and sometimes their very lives depended upon their vigilance. On this particular night, to them just like any other, they were on the job. Their vigil was a practical one, of being alert to prowlers, man or beast, who sought to rob or kill under cover of darkness. For this they were well prepared, but not for the angel, not for the radiance of God's glory, not for a night sky lit up by the hosts of heaven and certainly not for the amazing message they brought. The shepherds' reaction was one of terror, wonder and awe. Strong men who had faced wild beasts and brigands now shook with fear in the presence of these messengers of God who brought to them, not to the powerful and mighty, but to them, and to all those throughout the ages whom they represented – the poor, the marginalised, the abused, the forgotten – the song of hope, the good news of great joy that a Saviour had been born. They who had been faithful over little, that is, keeping watch over their flocks night after night, were now made faithful over much. They were moved up into the realm of mystery, to that spiritual dimension, entrusted with the greatest message of hope the world would ever receive. They had seen the invisible and touched the untouchable. The spiritual dimension became as real as the ordinary drudgery that filled their days, and life would never be the same. Throughout all the ages, these shepherds are remembered as 'vigil people' – people who kept watch and became bearers of a song of hope.

During Advent, the unseen world is breathtakingly, tantalisingly, close. Here in this cave now, for me, it is Advent. Many of us will, at least once, have experienced an ordinary day turned into an extraordinary one when we've been permitted to see beyond, to catch a glimpse of the something more, to hear a melody that causes our spirit to soar. We touch a mysterious reality accompanied by an awesome surge of hope. For example, I remember once standing in a *clochán* (a dry-stone hut used by early Christian religious orders, especially in County Kerry in Ireland) on the Dingle Peninsula, singing the doxology at the top of my voice and becoming conscious for a fleeting second of a vast, unseen chorus joining in. I realised then, as I do now in this cave, that I and we are not alone, abandoned or forgotten. I can see us surrounded by the great crowd of witnesses from every age and race who, empowered by the Spirit, were brave enough to dream, to listen to a melody other than the mournful dirge of self-interest, oppression and despair, and to sing out their song of hope. More often than not, their daring cost them their lives, but the melody remains for those with ears to hear, hearts to understand and spirits to join in.

It flashes into my mind, as it often has before, that God deliberately chose the peripheries of humanity for the birthplace of his Son. The first to announce the message of his birth brought by angels were these humble shepherds who carved out a meagre existence on the edge of society. Their journey led them from the humdrum and hardship of their marginalised, daily existence to a fleeting glimpse of glory, whose afterglow did not eliminate the drudgery but kept hope alive for all those who survive at the edges of life. I remember Bishop Trevor Huddleston, who worked in South Africa during the hard, cruel time of apartheid, asking why it was that the shepherds were the first at the stable. His answer to his own question came swiftly: because they were not afraid to bend and kneel. He meant this both literally and metaphorically, as the entrance to the cave or stable would have been low. Jesus, on his earthly journey, felt most at home with those on the margins of society. It is among such as these, who had nothing to lose and who could therefore be open to receiving in humility and with joy, that real community is most in evidence. It was on the margins that Jesus died, crucified between two thieves outside the walls of the Holy City, outside of all that seemed to matter in the eyes of the world.

I reflect that God, who is, in essence, the beloved community of Father, Son and Holy Spirit, delights in a diversity that constantly surprises us. I reflect that outsiders in such a kingdom become insiders. I reflect that these shepherds were numbered among the 'meek who shall inherit the earth'. I reflect that so much that I was not even aware of depends on us keeping watch. I reflect that the peace that God gives runs from the heart of the beloved through Bethlehem, Nazareth and the Via Dolorosa, and back to the heart where it all began. I hear the first faint notes of an outrageous song of hope. And I, too, am not afraid to bend and kneel.

It is hard to leave this place and return to the bustle of Bethlehem. But such is our schedule that it is not possible to linger long anywhere. (We do, however, have time to sample lunch in that restaurant that bears the name of Ruth!) Our next port of call is the Church of the Nativity, just around the corner from our hotel. Our group of pilgrims walks together to see the spot where it is believed that Jesus was born. We should have been prepared for the crowds and enormous queues, but they still take us by surprise. We need to be alert in order to stay together. This is a far cry from the experience of the shepherds! We shuffle forward a few paces and then stop. There are restoration works going on all around us; it is a bit like a building site. On one side, hiding some of the ongoing restoration, is a wall of canvas material. As people have waited their turn to go down to the grotto, they have signed the canvas and it is covered with signatures from all around the world. There is plenty of time to peruse it. Reading the canvas, listening to the babble of voices, I am reminded of the prophet Micah who said that, although Bethlehem was only a small village in Judah, from it there would come a ruler who would be the source of our peace. And he added, 'He will be highly honoured around the world.' I cannot help but think that this Scripture is fulfilled today, and every day, in this place.

At last we reach the entrance to the grotto. There is a sudden surge of people, all trying to get in first – no sense of community or humility here! I feel as though, if I paused at all, I would be trampled underfoot. Somehow this reinforces for me what I have read and heard of the disputes between the different Christian groups, jealous of each other's rights and claims upon various parts of this site. It smacks of power and control, almost a lusting after the biggest portion. I am reminded of the ancient bloody crusades, an attempt to guard these holy places for Christendom, and how the various participants believed that their involvement would earn them the approval of God or Allah. It seems to me that these modern quarrels or long-ago battles present an image to a watching world of faith that is more about external control and authority than the inner transformation that is the goal of any spiritual journey, leading as it should to a more just and compassionate world. 'Glory to God in highest heaven and on earth peace' is not the melody I am currently hearing. The very spot where we celebrate the birth of the Prince of Peace appears to be a place of unease and argument, of claiming rights and privileges, of pushing to be first in line. I don't know how it happens, but I find myself at the bottom of the steps and moving towards the special moment of placing my hand on the fourteen-pointed, silver star that marks the spot. I don't know what I expected to experience, but I am definitely not touched in my spirit or my emotions and move off to one side as quickly as possible. I feel disappointed and like an anonymous spectator, someone who is on the periphery of what is happening. This is for others – not for me.

Looking around at the crowds of people still pushing to get to this spot, I reflect that one of the questions plaguing me at times centres around awareness or awakening. Why do we close down on the unseen world that is all about us, that is waiting to break in at the point of awareness? What anaesthetises the spirit of daring to see beyond and, sometimes, in what may seem like moments of crazy abandonment, to journey towards the 'more' that, in a place beyond all formal knowing, we know is real? What blocks our ears so that we do not hear the song of hope that proclaims dawn is coming? Why am I not more awake? Perhaps part of the problem is that I think I need to be in a special place, both physically and spiritually, that I have to be feeling especially 'holy' – whatever that feels like. And yet, here I am in this special place and I feel nothing! But when I look to the Bible, I find that all the people called by God were not perfect, nor were they doing anything special when their moment of awakening came. They were just caught up in their everyday routine, like the shepherds.

It's so easy to fall into the trap of selective awareness. We may believe that we're alert but perhaps we simply see what we want to see and hear what we want to hear. It takes practice as well as desire to step back a little and simply be aware, to shed some of the baggage or conditioning that can colour our interpretation of what is unfolding before or within us. It is a choice to let go of the dualistic mindset that dominates so much of our thinking, seeing and doing, in order to take in the whole vista or panorama of a particular experience that spreads itself out before the gaze of our soul and our spirit. After we do step back, the call is to wait, not passively but passionately, for the sign or the whisper or the meaning – or the song.

This is difficult to convey because the sense of what I'm haltingly trying to express goes beyond even the loveliest of words; at best they can only approximate the meaning. For many years now I've had this sense of something more and it's still with me, perhaps beating more strongly in this phase of old age. It's not simply a yearning for the next life, for heaven, whatever we conceive heaven to be, but rather an ever-deepening awareness of the present moment, of the God who is always the 'I Am'. This God, in the 'present moments' of the years that have passed, has revealed something more of that essence of love when I've taken the time to be still and wait. One of the truths I've been alerted to, and am daily challenged to embrace more deeply, is that this God created and continues to create from a heart of loving diversity rather than of uniformity. We who have come from God and are returning to God are given this wonderful calling to explore, to experience, to embrace, to know again (which is the real meaning of 'recognise') that which we have 'forgotten' as we have grown older and become worldly-wise and have, perhaps, lost some of our trust and faith.

It is trust-filled waiting that we find so difficult, daring to hear the intriguing and alluring melody that is always present even though we don't usually recognise it, the breath of the Spirit that whispers to us of something more. We can talk quite readily about humankind pushing out the frontiers of knowledge in science and technology, or in space exploration, as we come to grips with some of the myriad wonders of the universe, but what about the frontiers of the Spirit? What about the endless possibilities and wonders, at the moment lying dormant within me and within you, that have never been explored? Are they waiting for an awakening, a moment of awareness, a new surrendering to God who is, in the end, the mystery of love? Can we really believe, really trust, that there is more to you, to me, even at this age and after all we have lived to date, than we have yet allowed ourselves to discover? Do we still have a song of hope? Obviously, many of these questions do not surface in my mind until long after we have left Bethlehem, but they were triggered by this particular visit.

Back in the grotto, our group finds a space a short distance from the scene of all the activity. We light some candles and begin to sing. Carols in June! ('Silent night, holy night – the dawn of redeeming grace.') Others not of our number are joining in. At last I have a sense of holy awe. This well-loved carol will never sound the same again. Someone strikes up another carol, 'O come, all ye faithful!' I thank God for all the faithful throughout two millennia, including those whom a few moments ago I dismissed so readily, who have come to Bethlehem, either in person or in spirit, and who know that what unites them is greater than all that would divide. 'O come, let us adore him, Christ the Lord.'

Are you a person who is awake and aware, someone
who can keep watch, or do you
find it hard?

Do you have within your spirit a hunger for
'something more'?

A PRAYER

Lord, thank you for songs to sing even in places of
uneasy peace. Wherever I find myself, may I let the
broken places within me and around me still sing
of your love and faithfulness. Let my life be a song
of hope. Amen.

CHAPTER SEVEN

A PLACE
CALLED HOME

Capernaum; Kursi

(*Luke 9:57–62; Mark 5:1–20*)

THE VERY NAME CAPERNAUM RESONATES WITH MUCH OF what we know of Jesus' ministry in Galilee. It is the beginning of another day and I am finding this visit especially fascinating. It would seem that Jesus made Peter's house his base. It was near the synagogue, and Capernaum itself was a thriving, busy, seaside town with fishermen, farmers, tax collectors, and the inevitable occupying forces – the Roman garrison. Jesus came here after his own home town, Nazareth, rejected him. There is so much to see and to absorb as ancient yesterday becomes today. The ruins of the synagogue and of Peter's house live again, both, in their own unique ways, centres of exuberant life and bustling activity. In fact, Peter's house seems to have been one of the more prosperous dwellings in the town. Obviously, if the catch was good, fishing paid well. I recall many characters and encounters associated with this place. Here in Capernaum a Roman officer, contrary to the stereotype, approached Jesus with humility and faith to plead for his gravely ill, beloved servant. As immediate healing flowed in response to a faith Jesus had not yet encountered in his ministry, he made his revolutionary declaration that the kingdom would embrace 'outsiders' from all over the world, while those who regarded themselves as insiders, with all their rights and privileges, might well be denied entry. Here in Capernaum Peter's mother-in-law was healed of a fever and it was to Peter's house that the crowds later flocked, clamouring and pleading for a touch or a healing word. Here in Capernaum a paralysed man responded to the free flow of forgiveness from Jesus and walked home carrying the mat where he had previously lain, immobile. Here in Capernaum Matthew, sitting in his tax collection booth as Jesus passed by, responded to his invitation and became one of the inner band of twelve. So Capernaum seems to be the hub of Jesus' ministry, the place that Jesus, for a brief period, called home.

The voice of our guide penetrates and we are back in today, obediently moving on to the next site. But as we are leaving, my attention is drawn to what appears to be a homeless man asleep on a bench. I draw closer and see that it is a bronze sculpture. I draw closer again and notice that while the head and hands are hidden in his outer garment, the feet are visible. And on the feet are nail prints – it is Jesus. I am told that this sculpture is called *Homeless Jesus*. It was designed by a Canadian sculptor, Timothy Schmalz. He offered it to St Michael's Cathedral in Toronto but it was declined, and then to St Patrick's Cathedral in New York, where it was also declined. Today there are over one hundred copies worldwide, including one outside Christ Church Cathedral in Dublin and one at the Salvation Army building in Belfast. It is specifically meant to challenge – it certainly challenges me. Even birds and animals seem to have a homing instinct, an innate drive that urges them to return to where they belong. I remember that it was here in Capernaum, in response to the teacher of religious law who, in the enthusiasm of the moment, declared he would follow him wherever he went, that Jesus said, 'Foxes have holes and the birds of the air have nests but the Son of Man has nowhere to lay his head.'

In today's world, probably more than at any other time in the history of humankind, there is a deep sense of loneliness, of lostness, of not belonging. This has become very apparent in the periods of lockdown necessitated by the COVID-19 pandemic. While people were largely confined to their houses or flats, these places of residence, if one were blessed enough to have a place of residence, did not necessarily convey the feeling of being 'at home'. Now, two years since the start of the pandemic, it is as if we are increasingly in exile from our true selves and having trouble finding our way 'back home'. By that I do not mean hankering for some past experience or place where we felt secure but rather what seems like an unattainable yearning to find or be found by someone or something in order to affirm us in who we really are. How do we reach the point of recognising that the way home is a forward motion that will, paradoxically, lead us back to where we started? And where we started was in the heart of God. As people of faith, we believe that we have come from God and we are returning to God. Our earthly experience is, for those who are aware, a journey in which we are challenged to be fully present *in* the world but also to be conscious of the fact that there is much more that we do not know, an unseen world, another dimension, and that what we experience here is but a dim image in a dusty mirror compared to what will one day be revealed. In that sense, we are all homeless. When we awaken to that fact, we may then be gifted with a deeper awareness of 'home' and the journey that must be made to get there. Often the only thing that keeps us going is the fleeting sense that there must be something more – to us, to life, to faith; a sort of homesickness for something that we knew once but have forgotten. Our new-found awareness is neither a conscious memory nor a mental image. Rather it is something that stirs our gut with varying degrees of intensity, sometimes causing us a deep, unspeakable longing and, at other times, to be filled with unspeakable joy when we catch a glimpse of the something more that somehow has a déjà vu ring to it.

Looking again at the sculpture of the homeless Jesus, I reflect that we most readily encounter the God of surprises when we are experiencing spiritual 'homelessness' in our lives. Maybe we only truly recognise those times in retrospect but it is actually in retrospect that they bless us. To be or to feel oneself homeless is always, in one way or another, to be on the margins, to be on the edge of society. I am very blessed in that I have never experienced actual physical homelessness but, as I have said, there are other experiences that can make us feel homeless or in exile of some sort or other, and I certainly have experienced those. Sometimes it has been a sense that I no longer belong in my particular religious denomination, that somehow I am on the periphery. Or it could be that the road taken arising out of my vocation has not been understood by others so that I feel pushed to the edges; sidelined. I immediately acknowledge that when I find myself in such a situation, it is partly 'they', those others, who have put me there, but also that I have put myself there, in my efforts to cope. Within all of us, I imagine, is a deep desire to belong, to know ourselves to be 'at home'. You may remember Robert Frost's poem 'The Death of the Hired Man', where he says, 'Home is the place where, when you have to go there, they have to take you in.' Then he adds, 'I should have called it something you somehow haven't to deserve.'* That is a pretty good description of grace. God chose the peripheries for the birthplace of his Son. Jesus, on his earthly journey, felt most at home with those living on the margins. And in him, margins become centres.

Viewed from afar, peripheries represent the unknown. Two of our most common reactions to such places are to fear them and/or to idealise them. Neither reaction is helpful nor does either represent the reality of those who, through no choice of their own or otherwise, are sentenced to exist on the fringes of their particular family or society. The Church has always preached about God hearing the cry of the poor and the importance of supporting the marginalised. But with ongoing accusations of irrelevancy, hypocrisy, ineffectiveness, abuse and betrayal, it seems that the Church itself has been ostracised to the margins, sent into exile, to the very place where it did not choose to go. And yet I believe that this can be a place of redemption and hope, where we are re-found by God and in turn find him among 'the least of these', where the prophetic voice is heard once again, where living the Beatitudes is paramount.

We see this, for example, in the work of Father Peter McVerry, who started his work in Ballymun in Dublin and whose trust, the Peter McVerry Trust, is now one of Ireland's largest organisations responding to homelessness, to those so obviously on the edge. It is not just that he heard the cry of the poor, of people who were actually homeless, but he has so identified with people living on the margins of society that he has become one of the foremost prophetic voices in Ireland today. The same is true of Capuchin Brother Kevin, who founded the Capuchin Day Centre in Dublin. And as I think more about the missionary orders or agencies of the different Churches, I know that so many of their members left 'home' in order to be present with, and for, marginalised people in many different countries. They risked not belonging, and that acute sense of homelessness that goes beyond the physical, in order to bring to others a sense of belonging and well-being, of respect and dignity. They have lived, and continue to live, as did the homeless Jesus, in solidarity with their sisters and brothers, part of a common humanity. They are both individually and collectively a prophetic voice that we would do well to listen to. When we experience a sense of not belonging, even if it is not actual physical homelessness, if we are awake to, and aware of, the experience, we may begin to become truly aware of our real 'home'. This home is not a distant, ephemeral heaven but something rooted in the eternal now of relationship. This is where Jesus chooses to be. This is where I remember what is most important. This is where margins become centres. This is where I am re-found by God and find him among the 'least of these'. Here in Capernaum the homeless Jesus, in whom all find their home, calls me again to come with him. I reluctantly leave the figure on the bench and join my fellow pilgrims as we leave the bustle of Capernaum and board the coach for our next visit.

We find ourselves in Kursi in the region of the Decapolis, what is known in the Gospels as the country of the Gerasenes. There are ruins of an old monastery and church but the rest of the area appears deserted. The limestone rocks are pockmarked with caves, many of which were used as tombs. Maybe it's because I know what happened here, namely the healing of the demon-possessed man and what tradition refers to as the 'miracle of the swine', that it all seems a bit eerie to me. I am sure the disciples felt the same when, after living through the storm at sea, they arrived here in the late evening and were immediately accosted by the screaming, naked figure emerging from the tombs. They were terrified, as was the whole surrounding countryside.

Desperately seeking shade from the sun, my companion and I stand in the shelter of some ruins as once again I see what's not there. I become one of the onlookers to an encounter that is very graphic and dramatic. The limestone rocks of Kursi were the land of this man's physical captivity, while the demon possession or insanity were his inner enslavement. He was most surely homeless in every sense of the word. He had lived among the tombs for years; no place called home for him. No one had been able to control him and the spin-off from his illness had resulted in his own greater destruction and being feared in the local community. But when mercy, justice, truth and peace in the person of Jesus met the community of demons – self-harm, destructive voices, blasphemy, violence, ignorance, hatred, fear – that had taken up residence within this man, they could not remain. The power and authority of such love rendered them impotent and the upshot was a man totally restored, clothed and in his right mind, sitting at the feet of Jesus. The community did not know how to respond to his restoration. It almost frightened them more than his madness. This seeming quiet could have been temporary – the demons could have taken over again at any moment. This prompted the crowd that had gathered to actually begin pleading with Jesus to go away and leave them alone. The man's insanity was what they had known for so long. They had coped with it by keeping their distance. How could they enter into relationship with someone transformed and what might this demand from them? Better the situation they knew, however scary and uncomfortable, than face something new.

Jesus was already in the boat when the man, probably sensing the mood of his neighbours, begged Jesus to let him come with him. But Jesus knew that the man had a new vocation now and pointed him towards it. His mission was to 'Go home and tell your friends what wonderful things God has done for you.' The man obeyed. He returned to the territory of the Decapolis and began to tell everyone about what Jesus had done for him. The next time Jesus visited this same area, crowds flocked to hear him speak and to beg for healing. The man had done his work well. His freedom led him to be available for their destiny, back where he once had been in chains. His encounter with Jesus truly had a multiple effect, which led many to encounter Jesus for themselves.

We are far from home in a land that is strange to us. Yet at this moment I am thinking of where I come from; where I live. Sometimes it is harder to recognise what God has done in the place we call home, where everybody thinks they know exactly who we are, allowing no room for growth or transformation. There is a sense that it is almost easier to be image-bearers of Jesus at the margins, on the peripheries, rather than at home where we are already boxed and labelled. In Ireland, it sometimes seems as if we have lived for centuries among the tombs of yesterday's dead and we banish those who are not like us to a place where we permit no possibility of change. Maybe collectively, especially in the North of Ireland, we have grown so accustomed to our demons that we wouldn't know who we were without them. They give us an identity, even if it is a negative one that at best can be embarrassing and at worst utterly tragic. The same is true of areas of internal conflict anywhere in the world – I know it is true of this land, Israel, as well. But there is an alternative, a new identity, a totally shared future, a place called home, that bears the hallmarks of mercy, justice, truth and peace. Perhaps such a choice evokes fear because of what it might demand of us? So we settle for less, until at last we are discarded and forgotten among the tombs of our own perpetuating, once again in a state of homelessness. In effect, we ask Jesus to leave us.

The only power that can make a difference is the power of infinite love that risks encounter, builds relationships and is open to forgiveness. All these things we find in Jesus. In the presence of such authority, fear, with its legion of 'demons', is rendered impotent. Saint Patrick in his latter years said that in his old age he wanted to do what he was unable to do in his youth, for he knew now what he should have done then. Retrospective guidance is a great thing! But the challenge is always in the present moment. For the pilgrims in our group, our particular country of the Gerasenes is Ireland and the choice is ours as to whether we ask Jesus to go away or beg him to stay.

What I know now, in this phase of my life, is that the biggest journey I will ever make is to come home to my true self. If we can discover, even a little, the transformation that comes from crossing the threshold, this will lead to a whole new vocation, to live the future we long for in the present moment. Do we have such a dream for Ireland, for this land where we are travellers passing through, for the Church, for the world, or are we in danger of choosing leaders who will only lead us back to slavery? In my old age, in all humility, I want to do what I was unable to do in my youth, partly because I lacked the courage to stand against some of the legion of demons, forgetting the promises of God. T.S. Eliot said, 'With the drawing of this Love and the voice of this Calling/We shall not cease from exploration.'** It is 'Love', i.e. God, who draws us as he repeatedly frees us from slavery in order to journey on to the next threshold, to find that place called home; it is the voice, the whisper of this 'Calling', this vocation to behold God in the wonderful unity of his loving diversity, that sustains and encourages us on our journey. No longer bound by the chains of our past, nor enticed repeatedly to dwell among the tombs of yesterday, but clothed in right relationships, we become that sign of hope for the world that has always been our destiny as people of Ireland, but until now unfulfilled. And I know that there are many in this land who sense a similar destiny for this beautiful, tortured, divided country.

As we board our coach again, I find I am carrying a burden of sadness for the times when we, as communities, have effectively asked Jesus to leave us. But I also give thanks for individuals who never give up, who live out the freedom they have experienced, who do their work well and are a sign of hope for the world and who point us to a place called home that paradoxically is here in the eternal now of presence.

*   Robert Frost, 'The Death of the Hired Man', *Complete Poems of Robert Frost* (New York: Holt, Reinhart and Winston, 1949), p. 53.
** T.S. Eliot, 'Little Gidding', *Four Quartets* (London: Faber and Faber Ltd., 1959), p. 48.

What does the word 'homesickness'
evoke for you?

Looking back, where or when have
you felt most at home?

A PRAYER

Lord, make me more aware of the plight of the
homeless in our society.

For the times in my life when, either through my
words, attitudes or actions I have asked you to
leave, have mercy. Lord, you are my true home. I
pray that you will always find your home in me.
Amen.

CHAPTER EIGHT

WELCOME!

Jericho

(*Luke 10:30–37;*
Luke 19:1–10)

THE AIR-CONDITIONED COACH IS HURTLING ON ITS WAY
from Jerusalem to Jericho. South of Jerusalem, the terrain
quickly takes on the mantle of desert: dry, rocky little bits
of scrub and the occasional Bedouin camp with makeshift
shacks, a few goats, the odd television aerial or battered
car. Suddenly, about 17 km from the city, I notice a sign
pointing to the Good Samaritan Inn. Now, I know that
this is not actually an inn but a museum of mosaics and
various items from archaeological digs, some dating from
the first century BC. But it is conceivable that there was
an inn near here in Jesus' day. This road was notorious
for ambush and robbery. And Jesus must have walked
this route many times. All of this could have formed the
dramatic backdrop to the story Jesus told in response to
the question 'Who is my neighbour?' As probably the
best-known and most loved of all the parables, we may
be very familiar with how it begins: 'A man was going
down from Jerusalem to Jericho and fell into the hands

of robbers who stripped him, beat him, and went away, leaving him half dead.' It almost has a 'Once upon a time' storytelling feel to it. We think we know it inside out. But did you ever think about the inn?

On this journey I can imagine how difficult such a trek would have been in Jesus' time, not only because of the merciless heat with no prospect of shade, but the danger from bandits who would quickly swoop down on any unsuspecting traveller, taking what they wanted and leaving the victim like a heap of litter by the roadside. On this particular occasion, we know what happened – how it was the third passer-by, the stranger, the 'enemy', the Samaritan, who stopped, went above and beyond with generosity and compassion, and took the wounded man to a nearby inn. What is remarkable about this is that everyone who heard Jesus tell this story knew that Jews and Samaritans had absolutely no dealings with each other. They were sworn enemies. So you can imagine what a risk Jesus was taking when he made the Samaritan, the Jewish traveller and the innkeeper the chief protagonists in his story. The priest and the Levite, the 'important' people who passed by, were relegated to the sidelines, of no significance except for highlighting the extraordinary actions of the stranger, so different to their own. In my imagination, the three characters move out of the shadows and become real. I want to know what happened to the wounded man, how the innkeeper dealt with him after his benefactor left and, most of all, did the stranger return and did he find a whole new chapter emerging out of his selfless act of compassion?

First and foremost, the inn's purpose was as a place of hospitality. In ancient times, all travellers depended on someone else's hospitality. Ancient Israelites understood themselves as strangers and sojourners, therefore it was incumbent upon them to care for vulnerable strangers in their midst. This was part of what it meant to be the people of God. And today there are still many here who express their faith through life in community, shared prayer, hospitality and healing, these being the ways in which they seek to manifest the love of God in the world. The inn certainly embodied at least some of these values, and perhaps the others emerged as host and guest became better acquainted. The whole concept of hospitality is at the core of the Gospel, hospitality between us and God, between the alienated parts of our own inner beings, between ourselves and others, and between ourselves and all creation. The inn in this particular story became the ultimate symbol of safety and hospitality. In the ancient Middle East, if someone came across an encampment or an inn while fleeing from an enemy, it was incumbent upon the host to welcome the stranger and, while he was in receipt of this hospitality, his enemy could not touch him. So we find in Psalm 23: 'You prepare a banquet for me where all my enemies can see me. You welcome me as an honoured guest and fill my cup to the brim.'

The Samaritan traveller and the Jewish innkeeper joined forces to aid the wounded man. I imagine that, once the man became a little stronger, he would have started sharing a little bit of himself with the innkeeper and the innkeeper with him. They would have listened to each other. This is one of the most precious gifts we can offer anyone. When we award people the dignity and respect of really hearing what they are saying, and even what they are not saying, when they know that someone believes them and takes them seriously, that is very often where the process of transformation begins. Over the years in Restoration Ministries (the organisation with which I work), we have sought to exercise this sort of hospitality and to provide just such a safe place where people can come and tell their stories and really be heard. We have learned that genuine listening requires an openness of mind, generosity of heart, humility of spirit and the courage to be vulnerable before others, all of which are hallmarks of the beloved community. Under the umbrella of hospitality, a guest should expect to find not only security and generosity but also a spirit of rest and healing. The Samaritan who brought the wounded Jew to the roadside inn portrayed this generosity in the extreme, being willing to pay whatever was necessary, and more, so that everything possible might be done to aid the man's recovery.

Perhaps that generosity was contagious for the innkeeper as he stepped into the role of carer and did his best to make his inn a place of recovery. For that is what it was, or should have been, a place of restoration and reconciliation, where people who are weary from their journey through life, who are feeling lost, or lonely, or without a sense of belonging, who have a broken self-image or have broken relationships with others, or who feel actively pursued by hatred or despair, can enter and find rest and peace and healing. After tending the man overnight, the Samaritan handed the innkeeper the equivalent of two full days' wages to cover the patient's upkeep. 'If you spend more than that,' he said, 'I will repay you the next time I'm passing.' And off he went, seeking neither recognition nor thanks. The inn also became a place of celebration and of community: as he recovered, the wounded man and the innkeeper would have grown together in trust, maybe they would have talked about the Samaritan stranger and how his actions had jolted their prejudices and burst open some of their unexploded myths about the other. What a road of reconciliation they had begun to travel because one man had acted as neighbour to the perceived 'enemy'. It was almost as if the Samaritan had left something of his presence with them, like a precious fragrance. And how they must have eagerly scanned the horizon for his return, to hear his story and discover in greater depth what it would mean for him to 'spend more'.

As the coach hurtles on towards Jericho, not a bandit in sight, I find myself asking the question, 'Where are today's inns?' Are they our churches? Do we find them on the roadside of life, open to receive and welcome those who need a resting place or a place of safety or healing, for whatever reason? Are they communities of celebration? Do people find in them the challenge and the means through which they can be reconciled, not only with God, but also with their own inner beings and with one another? Does the traveller sense flowing from them a generosity of spirit, a willingness to spend more, more of themselves, more of their resources, more of their faith, so that all who pass by are not only welcomed but restored in order that they may continue on their journey? Are they so pervaded by the presence of Jesus (so often the 'stranger' to our cherished way of being and doing) that something of his fragrance lingers in their very atmosphere?

One of my favourite places is the sacred space of the abbey on the island of Iona. The founder of the Iona Community, George MacLeod, regarding its beauty as a restored place of pilgrimage sanctified by all the prayers of the centuries, said, 'It's not just the interior of these walls: it's our own inner beings you have renewed. We are your Temple not made with hands. We are your body. If every wall should crumble and every church decay, we are your habitation.'* We are the Church. So I need to look beyond the Churches of which I and possibly you are a part, and ask deeper, more intimate, personal questions. Am I an inn? Am I, in my very self, a resting place of safety and hospitality for others? Is generosity a way of life for me? What are the laws of hospitality that rule my life? Have I been so attentive to my own inner journey on which I am called to the creation of the beloved community within that I am always prepared to let go and unlearn in order to embrace and be embraced by the stranger, the unseen guest, and by the mystery of the sacred now?

The only way in which I can even begin to approach such a way of being is if I allow the inn of abiding to develop within me. If there is within me a place of prayer, a place of deep communion and intimacy, a place where Jesus is present and welcome, then, however stumblingly, I begin to become that roadside inn. This is something that does not happen overnight, but takes years of perseverance and even then we are only just beginning. Somehow I feel that I need to have these truths emphasised again and again until they become second nature and find an abiding place deep within me. Little do I know that before this day has ended I will have had my half-formed prayer granted.

These are the thoughts that accompany me as we literally come down into Jericho, described as the city of palm trees. It is the lowest permanently inhabited city on earth and believed to be the oldest continuously inhabited city in the world. On this occasion, our focus of interest is not so much the city as a sycamore tree, described in the guide book as Zacchaeus' tree. It is a very old tree but I know it cannot possibly be the one that the unpopular tax collector, collaborator with the occupying Roman forces, cheater of the poor, climbed that day long ago. The coach stops on the other side of a busy road. We cross over and stand under the tree as we listen to our guide. Someone reads the story of the encounter between Jesus and Zacchaeus from Luke's Gospel.

The name Zacchaeus means the 'pure and blessed one'; however, he was anything but! Despised and shunned, for years he had sought his identity and security in ways that had alienated him not only from others but also from his true self. He was competent in his work; he was wealthy and successful. But nothing could assuage the loneliness, the fear, the shame, that lay below the exterior image. Zacchaeus had a home but he didn't really know, had never experienced, what it meant to be 'at home'. He didn't have a true sense of identity. He didn't know what it was to be confronted and embraced by love. He basically didn't know who he was. So there is a sense in which he was an orphan, carrying with him all the negativity that such a label can convey. But on this particular day something stirred inside him when he heard the news, via the gossip of the crowded streets, that Jesus would be passing through. There was an inexplicable urge within him to see this itinerant preacher he'd heard about, but he didn't want to be seen. He risked the ridicule of the crowds: his solution was to climb a tree. Looking at this tree that we have been brought to, I can see that it would have been possible for someone who wasn't very tall, as

Zacchaeus was described, to climb up and hide among its leafy branches.

In his public ministry, Jesus often passed a particular way as if the sole purpose of his journey was to meet a specific individual; the time and place were unknown to the individual in question but were set by divine appointment. Such a one was his encounter with Zacchaeus. The noise of the modern traffic fades into the background. Once again, I see what's not there. I am back on the crowded streets of centuries ago. The little man hiding in the tree feels pretty confident that he can't be seen. But the sudden stillness from below alerts him. The crowd has stopped and someone is calling him by name. 'Zacchaeus, come down for I must be a guest in your house today.' Before they are even introduced, Jesus knows his name and where he is, and invites himself into Zacchaeus' home and life. The tax collector throws caution to the winds. He hurriedly scrambles down and excitedly brings Jesus to his home. I reflect that Zacchaeus had to climb down in order to meet with Jesus. His outer garments of power, wealth and officialdom were cast aside. He was, in a sense, naked before Jesus. And it didn't bother him. He had been seen, not with contempt, accusation or hatred but, for once, with love and compassion, a love that restored his true dignity and identity. What always intrigues me is what we are not told, namely about the private encounter and conversation in Zacchaeus' home that led to such a change in him. It is rightly shrouded in the intimacy of silence, but the results are there for all to see and to wonder at. Zacchaeus, having welcomed Jesus not only into his house but, much more importantly, into the home of his heart, was totally transformed. His immediate declarations bore witness to this fact. Jesus publicly reinstated him into the family of God, to his rightful place: Zacchaeus now belonged and, from that new-found identity, his generosity overflowed. In fact, through what he said then and his subsequent actions, Zacchaeus reclaimed his name as the pure and blessed one. I recall the Beatitude 'Blessed are the pure in heart for they shall see God' (Mt 5:8). Zacchaeus saw God and God saw him – a mutual recognition with a wonderful outcome.

I realise that I am being told something yet again. It was brought strongly to my attention earlier when I saw the sign for the Good Samaritan Inn and now, just in case I haven't got the message, here it is again! The something I am being told is that the only way for Jesus to be a guest in the home that is me is if I, too, come down from my metaphorical tree. Often I find it difficult to do that, to let go of the busyness, the worries, the plans, the cares that overcrowd each day, leaving no space to simply be. I tend to have an approach-avoidance attitude to being invited to 'let go'. Perhaps I am apprehensive about the intimacy of silence. Yet I also know that it is in those times when I consent to such a state that a shift or change can take place within me. In other words, when I give up some of my control and my agenda and simply make space for Jesus and welcome him, the transforming power of love can have its way with me.

From the vantage point of 2022, the darkness of pandemic lockdown has given us just such a space, even if it has been an unwelcome guest. I have prayed over this period that I would not miss the treasure hidden in the field of lockdown. The challenges have not been comfortable and my resistance to some of them has left me feeling, at times, that I am back behind the starting line. But I do know now, without a shadow of a doubt, that two of the most important clues in the treasure hunt are to wait and listen. Some early Christian mystics describe what happens when we pursue such a path, the path of going deeper in our relationship with God, as being so 'widened' by our waiting that it changes our 'wanting'. It is about letting go rather than holding on. It is about unlearning rather than seeking to learn. It is about handing over control of who we are to God, consenting to his presence and action within, so that our true self, as opposed to our smaller self or ego, may gradually emerge and know herself part of the beloved community of the Trinity.

It is a journey that will take more than a lifetime, but each time we come to God with no agenda save an awareness of being in the presence of the beloved, I believe there is a shift in the unseen world towards inclusion, unity and peace. My limited experience has been that this awareness, born out of the intimacy of silence, spills over from such practice into ordinary daily living, just as it did with Zacchaeus. I know that as I faithfully commit to such a journey I will find that I no longer need to cling to the various defence mechanisms that have been the source of my security for far too long. It is a process of 'coming down'. Through recognising the fact that I belong and that I am loved, any sense of non-being is replaced by a humility that enables me to live with a newfound compassion and awareness. As I see and am seen, I awaken to the welcome that has a limitless embrace. I know somewhere deep within me that everything belongs. Infinite love is continually calling me and naming me.

Returning to that particular day of pilgrimage, I am glad that I saw the sign for the Good Samaritan Inn. I am glad for the challenge of radical hospitality. I am glad we have come down to Jericho. I am glad we have seen this tree that both is and is not Zacchaeus' tree. I am glad to have been so visibly reminded of the invitation to come down and, in so doing, to grow ever more deeply into an image bearer of welcome, welcoming Jesus, welcoming myself, welcoming the other and welcoming this beloved creation. I will not forget this day!

---

* George F. MacLeod, *The Whole Earth Shall Cry Glory* (Isle of Iona: Wild Goose Publications, 1985), p. 45.

Are you, in yourself, an inn, a place of welcome, a
place of abiding?

What happens when you 'come down'; when you
let go and simply 'be'?

A PRAYER

Lord, you rejoiced in welcoming those who were
different, those on the edge. Through you, with
you and in you, outsiders become insiders; margins
become centres. And you welcome me! May my life
bear witness to such welcome. Amen.

CHAPTER NINE

Blessed are
the merciful

YOU ARE
BLESSED

Pool of Bethesda;
Mount of Beatitudes

(John 5:1–13; Matthew 5:1–11)

THIS MORNING WE BOARD THE COACH OUTSIDE OUR
hotel on the outskirts of the Holy City very early. Today
is going to be busy. We soon have one visit behind us as
we emerge from the silence and coolness of the beautiful
Church of St Anne in Jerusalem into the stark contrast
of bright, almost blinding, sunlight and the excited
chatter of different groups of pilgrims. The church is
believed to be built over the cave/house where the Virgin
Mary's parents, Anne and Joachim, lived. It has a special
ambience, perhaps due partly to its lack of adornment
and its wonderful acoustics. It is still early morning and
our next destination is within walking distance. Our
spiritual accompanier finds us a quiet corner by the Pool
of Bethesda near the Sheep Gate, where we can observe
the ruins of this once bustling focal point; this age-old
place of asylum and healing. In ancient times, crowds of
sick people could be found here every day. They believed
that this was a healing spring. If they managed to get into

the water when it was stirred (according to tradition, by an angel), they might experience a miracle. Over centuries, the healing spring of water, the 'Pool', has disappeared. All that is left is a dry gully and the crumbling ruins of the elegant pillars forming part of the five covered porches that provided asylum for those who sought it.

I seek to move to a different space inside myself, to use my sanctified imagination, to see what is no longer there. I allow the chatter going on around me to become the noise of many voices from long ago, belonging to the throngs who flocked here. I hear arguments, excitement, groans, begging; expressions of cynicism, disbelief, expectancy; everyday concerns all vying with each other to be the loudest voice. Unexpressed, but there nonetheless, are also the desperate hopes of the seemingly incurable for whom this place of asylum existed. One meaning of the name Bethesda is 'house of mercy'. I reflect that every day on our pilgrimage we are reminded of mercy through Mary's wonderful song of praise to God who is the faithful mercy-giver, because every morning, once we settle ourselves in the coach, we say the Magnificat together as part of the Morning Prayer of the Church. Perhaps the loudest cry that sounded from this place, either voiced or as a silent scream, was for mercy and, among the cries, that of a man who had been paralysed for thirty-eight years. I reflect that, as Jesus walked among the ill and marginalised of society, his attention was arrested by this man, as if he had come specifically and solely for him.

What a day this was for this unnamed man! He had been carried as usual to the same place, to wait with little expectancy for a moving of the waters. All he could see were the feet of those strolling or rushing past. No one took any notice of him; no one, that is, until a pair of feet stopped beside him and didn't move on. He had no idea what was about to unfold. Healing was no problem for Jesus. The problem lay with the man: does he want to be well, or had he either lost hope or become so at home with his condition that he wouldn't know who he was without it? In the man's response Jesus heard the cry for mercy and spoke the life-giving word. Immediately the man got up, picked up his sleeping mat, and walked.

The question Jesus asked the man, 'Would you like to get well?', has always challenged me. I think about myself and how resistant I can sometimes be to change. Do I really want it? I can too easily cling to the familiar, to the security of how things have always been, and allow the fear of the unknown hold me back. I can blame my lack of growth on the fact that there is, for me, no equivalent of an angel to 'stir up the water'. At the same time there is part of me that really wants to move forward, to risk uncharted territory, to be more whole, to be 'well'. I look around at my fellow pilgrims and reflect that this is probably also true of them. In fact, both an individual and collective cry for mercy arises from the whole of humankind, whether voiced or not. Many are totally imprisoned by their situations, like the man by the pool.

There are lives full of anguish, desperation, poverty and oppression on a scale I can hardly imagine. Others, like myself, simply need the courage and the faith to choose the unfamiliar way. As I linger by the ruins of Bethesda, I know that the mercy-giver hears my cry. 'Lord Jesus Christ, Son of the Living God, have mercy on me!'

I turn to follow the others back to the coach, but my attention is arrested by a sizeable group of young clerics, all arrayed in severe black, looking very serious and important as they peer over the balustrade at the site of the pool below. Even at this hour the heat is blistering and I wonder how they bear it with their heavy raiment. Perhaps it is simply association of ideas, but I think of the Jewish leaders, serious and important, who had their spies in the crowd, seeking to find something to pin on Jesus to discredit him, because they could not cope with his ministry and the appeal he had for the people. This time he had broken the rules by healing on the Sabbath. They thought they had finally got him! This was not actually the case, but it increased their desire to have him killed. He disturbed their man-made order and could not be allowed to continue. I recall with some sadness the disturbing current trend within various branches of the Christian Church to promote its idea of order, accompanied by exhortations to adhere to multiple rules and regulations as a condition of being accepted into the body. If followed to the letter, this effectively wipes out the wonderful values of inclusion, openness and unity as well as the richness of diversity in favour of a suffocating uniformity and a striving for 'purity'. It also, by and large, does away with mercy, so desperately needed today and yet, so often, in such short supply. Some of those same Jewish leaders might have been among those who later stood near the cross as Jesus was dying. They would have heard his words, 'Father, forgive them. They don't know what they're doing.' Final words of mercy that opened up a new beginning for all of humankind; I wonder did they really hear them? But I need to hurry now to catch up with my fellow pilgrims. I take a last glance at the group of earnest young men still looking at the pool named the 'house of mercy' and I pray for myself and for them that God will always lead us out into the wide, open spaces of his love and mercy.

'Surely goodness and mercy shall follow me' could sum up most of my experience of this pilgrimage. I am daily reminded in so many ways of the goodness of God and the word 'mercy' does indeed seem to be pursuing me here. It is strongly reinforced for me on a visit we made another day, to the Mount of Beatitudes. There are many mountains and hills in the Holy Land but this hill holds a special place in my heart. Before setting out on this pilgrimage there were two experiences I earnestly wished to have: one, already mentioned, a boat trip on the Sea of Galilee, and the other a visit to this alluring and sacred spot, believed to be the site of the Sermon on the Mount. Once out of the coach, I feel a thrill of excitement as we move through the entrance to the site. It is as if we are entering another world. All of my senses have a heightened awareness. Everything is breathtakingly beautiful – the scent and sight of flowers, the sparkling waters of the Sea of Galilee below, the sound of birdsong sweeter than any choir and, later, the touch of peace and the taste of bread and wine at the Eucharist in the garden of the Church of the Beatitudes. It seems fitting that it is a branch of the Franciscans that has developed and preserved this lovely place. It is their founder who urges us to recognise all of creation, including humankind, as being united in its diversity, praising God. Everything and everyone is called to be in relationship, in harmony. Everything belongs!

I find it almost incredible to think that I am actually here, making the same ascent as Jesus and his friends, women and men, did all those centuries ago. We modern-day pilgrims from all over the world follow a carefully laid-out walkway up the gentle slopes. I wonder how many of my fellows have been captivated, as I have been throughout my life, by the timeless words, the first of the eight Beatitudes: 'Blessed are the poor in spirit for theirs is the Kingdom of Heaven.' In effect, Jesus is saying, 'This is what you sign up for if you choose to come with me. Let this be the way you live your life. Let this be your attitude.' Jesus embodies in himself each of these challenges along with their accompanying blessings.

Stone tablets are placed equidistantly from each other along the walkway, each carved with a Beatitude. I pause and read each of them as if for the first time. My overwhelming desire is to remain in this beautiful place for much longer than our scheduled time. One could spend days just reflecting on these hallmarks of what it means to be a citizen of the kingdom. But that is not possible on a pilgrimage like this. There are always other places to go and more to see and experience. I do actually stop for a few minutes at the fifth tablet: 'Blessed are the merciful for mercy will be shown to them.' It's that word again – mercy.

Mercy (in Hebrew *hesed*) is one of the great words of the Bible. I reflect that it is one of the most used words for maybe the least practised value within the institutional Church. Throughout the ages, and daily around the world, the words 'Lord, have mercy' form an integral part of worship. *Hesed* is sometimes translated as 'loving kindness' and sometimes as 'steadfast love'. It incorporates healing and freedom, forgiveness and compassion, and describes the character of God's dealing with humankind throughout history. This is the God who, in the ultimate act of mercy, sends his Son because we could not cure our own wounded condition. In Jesus we recognise the true nature of the Father's heart and, from the cross, a tidal wave of mercy flows for all people, for all time, including for me and my fellow travellers.

All of us, without exception, have been recipients of mercy whether we were conscious of it or not. I know that God has answered this cry from my heart even when I could not put words to the pleading. Why, then, am I sometimes so slow to be a mercy-giver? Why is my own life not bent towards mercy in the same way as God's heart is bent towards me? At the heart of this fifth Beatitude lies the challenge to be generous of spirit, to be compassionate, to identify with those who are defenceless, who are victims of their own or others' wrongdoing. It is an attitude that requires decision as well as feeling. It is a call to care passionately, even for those who have wronged me or whom I don't naturally like. It is also a challenge to be merciful towards myself, for I know that I often reserve the harshest judgement for my own, at times, confused and troubled being. I have often witnessed a process of transformation in those who open themselves up to the practice of mercy. If we do commit to such a journey, then both our inner and outer worlds will manifest the hallmarks of the kingdom. A new community of mercy-givers and -receivers can change the Church, can change Ireland, can change the world. These are the thoughts that surge in my mind to such a degree that it wouldn't take much prompting for me to shout them from the top of this mountain!

But I need to move; I am causing a bit of a traffic jam. For the moment, I set mercy aside. When I come to the tablet with the seventh Beatitude, I become acutely aware that, for me at least, one Beatitude follows on almost naturally from the other, building up to a crescendo in the seventh: 'Blessed are peacemakers for they shall be called the children of God.' Once again I come to a halt. I know from first-hand experience that peacemaking can be a messy business and is not the same as peace-loving. There is a vast difference between the two. I can love and yearn for peace from the security of my own 'camp'; my own tribe or culture. But to be a peacemaker demands that I get involved, that I risk, that I cross boundaries into hitherto unknown territory. I may have to make some tough decisions that will lead to misunderstanding, rejection, even alienation, especially from those who assume I am on their 'side'. To embrace such a challenge, to keep on building relationships, finding common ground, refusing to label or write people off, always seeking to find something that unites rather than seizing upon that which divides, allowing myself to be stretched beyond where I feel I can be stretched, trying always to point to windows of hope in places of despair: all of this can take its toll. And I know that the promised blessing can create for the peacemaker many enemies. So, on this perfect day, in this perfect place, I take serious note of the Beatitude preceding the seventh. The sixth tablet names as blessed those who are pure in heart, the promise to them being that they shall see God. It's as if we are being prepared for number seven!

First and foremost, I need to become a person of peace within myself. That will only happen if I take time to nurture my friendship with Jesus by discovering the secret of mutual abiding. Such freedom comes from the realisation that it is not about doing more but simply about being. When such a point of stillness is reached, barely perceptibly can grow within us a unity that transcends the menacing 'either/or' struggle that can dominate much of life. This stillness stems from the flow or communion between me and the one who loves me. In such a sacred space, striving withers up and dies and, in its place emerges, in all its gently refined beauty, what Jesus calls purity of heart. This is possible for anyone. Without such nurturing or desire, I know that I will be lured off the path by all sorts of false promises and temptations to shortcuts that lead only to chaos. But as the mutuality of belovedness deepens, we 'see' more clearly. In knowing who we are in Jesus, we begin to see him in others, also. We start to trust in a whole new way. As we let go of attitudes that have trapped and cluttered us, we become more aware, we detect deeper meaning, and we receive the promise. We 'see' God. When we experience this, we are on our way to becoming channels of peace and will, ourselves, possess an inner peace that remains with us, no matter what storms we face in responding to the challenge to be peacemakers.

The promise, the blessing that comes from this Beatitude, is amazing. We are called, accepted, known as children of God, as God's friends. And one of the wonderful things about such a calling is that we are welcomed into a huge, united, yet very diverse, family. I get a hint of this as I look around at all the pilgrims from so many different nations who have chosen to visit this holy place. I'm somewhat reluctant to move on to the eighth and final Beatitude for I know that to commit to the calling of peacemaking will inevitably involve persecution. The temptation is for me to say yes to all the other Beatitudes – but not this one. I arrive at the eighth Beatitude at last, 'Blessed are those who are persecuted for the sake of righteousness, for theirs is the kingdom of heaven.' My doubts and questions fall into a vibrant and overwhelming silence filled with the presence of a God who is not remote but who chooses to be near, knowing what it will cost. This is the God who sweats blood in a garden and earnestly prays that he will not have to be persecuted for the sake of righteousness. This is the God who willingly climbs another hill and finds there not acclamation but a cross. This is the God who not only submits but embraces such a path, all for righteousness' sake – for restored relationships. This is the path walked by Jesus who incarnates all these Beatitudes in his own person. This is the blessed one.

We have reached the summit of what is really little more than a large hill. I am glad that we are given some time to be alone to absorb the beauty but also, and more crucially, to reflect on the calling to be a person who lives the Beatitudes. Later, as we gather to worship in the open air, feeling at one with all creation and bathed in the mercy of God, it is fitting that the song chosen is one attributed to Saint Francis of Assisi. We join with the rest of creation in this place of breathtaking beauty as we sing, 'Make me a channel of your peace.'

Would you like to be 'well'?
What would this mean for you?

What does mercy say to you?

A PRAYER

Lord Jesus Christ, Son of the living God,
have mercy on me.

And let me sow love instead of hate, pardon instead
of injury, faith instead of doubt. May I bring hope
into places of despair, light into darkness, joy into
sadness. Make me an instrument of your peace.
Amen.

CHAPTER TEN

A LOVE STORY

Jordan River; Mount Tabor

(*Matthew 3:13–17;*
Matthew 17:1–8)

AT THE END OF MATTHEW'S GOSPEL, BEFORE JESUS
takes his leave of the disciples and ascends to the Father,
he commissions them to go into the world proclaiming
the Good News, making new disciples and baptising
them in the name of the Father and the Son and the
Holy Spirit. Then he assures them of his continuing,
abiding presence. So today we are at the banks of the
Jordan River, at a site believed to be the place where
Jesus was baptised by John. We are being given the
opportunity to renew our baptismal vows and to descend
into the water, as thousands or millions of people have
done before us throughout the centuries since the day
when Jesus himself went in. It was here, as he emerged
from the baptismal waters, that John saw the Spirit of
God descending upon Jesus in the form of a dove and
heard the words, 'This is my beloved Son and I am fully
pleased with him.' This was Jesus 'going public'; the
beginning of his ministry. It was here that he received

the seal of approval from the Father and was assured of his belovedness.

I suppose I should feel some sense of holy awe or spiritual excitement. Instead, I merely feel a little apprehensive as we are assigned towels and white gowns and pointed towards changing rooms before proceeding to the space allotted to our group at the water's edge. I have no sense of the sacred, more a feeling of being on a conveyer belt, and just wish it was over. Should I turn back? I wade into the water. Just behind is my close friend and colleague. She is Catholic, black, and Nigerian; I am Protestant, white, and Irish. The priest from our group and the pilgrimage leader are waiting. I move forward – 'In the Name of the Father and of the Son and of the Holy Spirit' – and three times I am immersed in the waters of the Jordan. My friend follows. We come up out of the water together, hand in hand, singing. The medieval proverb about blood being thicker than water refers to family connection, loyalty and bonding. But in baptism, water is 'thicker' than blood. We receive a whole new kinship in Christ. Later, after a short liturgy, we will receive certificates stating that we renewed our vows at the Jordan. But I know that I won't need a certificate to remind me of the irrevocable truth I carry away with me. As I look at the baptismal stations along this stretch of the river, I realise that all these people, wherever they come from, however they express their faith, are my sisters and brothers. And I think of what a different place this world would be if Christians lived out of such truth and such convictions.

But there is more. For years I have been fascinated and intrigued by the word 'beloved', the word spoken at Jesus' baptism. It is an old word. It is a profoundly intimate word. You have only to read the Song of Songs to understand this. The English language does not have as many words denoting nuances of difference in the concept of love as others do, especially, perhaps, those languages that originate in Latin. For me, 'beloved' carries with it both a particularity and a universality. I love words and I love finding out all I can about them and, in order to plumb their depths a little, I love analysing them. I think this word, beloved, tops the list for me. We tend to regard it as an adjective describing someone who is very dear, or a noun that simply denotes a much-loved other. But when you break the word down, what do you get? 'Be loved.' So it is also a word that evokes energy, action, movement, growth. It actually can be a challenge, a command, even a vocation, especially the vocation to love ourselves. Lest you think this smacks of pride and self-importance, not so; to truly love yourself as the unique and special creation that you are leads rather to huge gratitude for the gift and a deep humility for what has been given. Due to both nature and nurture, many of us have a hard job in believing or recognising that we are capable of loving and of being loved. Experience, so we think, has taught us that this is not possible. We can be weighed down by feelings of low self-worth, of rejection, of loneliness and not belonging, of feeling that we don't really matter to anyone. We can so easily fall into the trap of thinking ourselves invisible. These types of feelings may have taken such deep root within us that we regard them as irreversible truth, which can often result in an outlook on life that is suffused with self-pity or barely controllable anger. We may even hate ourselves, or who we believe ourselves to be. As a consequence, we may base our lives on being busy in order to avoid thinking or reflecting too much. Or we can become caught in the trap of people-pleasing as the only way to be accepted.

The trouble is that, without the assurance of being loved, there is a bottomless pit inside us and so whatever we do, or seek to be, it's never enough. We end up in the same place of hopelessness and of feeling marginalised, even after all our efforts. No wonder that many look to an external source to give them an identity and feeling of worth. It may be a gang or a paramilitary group, or a political party, or something that appears more innocent, like a football supporters club. We may look to our different Church institutions to give us identity and self-worth. We obey the rules and regulations of the group to the letter. We may, sadly in some cases, be prepared to die for them. I am convinced that the major source of conflict in the world stems from not being able to love oneself or having the assurance of being loved. But once we begin to see differently, things start to shift a little. We will have begun a journey that will enable us, with quiet assurance and humility, to take our place within a common humanity. And not only that, we will begin to see others not as threats or aliens but as our sisters and brothers.

I have had a dream of community all my adult life. This is not something I have conjured up. Rather it feels as if it was given to me; revealed, if you like. Over time, it has changed in appearance; it has grown and been enriched by encounters with those who in themselves were image bearers of the dream. But in essence it has remained the same. I call it the 'beloved community'. I first came across that name when I was twenty-one years old. Now I am elderly, but the drumbeat remains, leading me where I sometimes haven't wanted to go, honing my thought processes and, indeed, my whole inner being. From this vantage point, I see that the drumbeat was not that of a solo player but was, in fact, its source; it is community itself, the beloved community of the Trinity, Father, Son and Holy Spirit. The particularity of knowing oneself beloved leads to the commonality of belovedness. I sense, by the waters of the Jordan, that it is no accident that this word, beloved, is used right at the start of Jesus' public ministry, not only as assurance for him, and maybe for his cousin John, but also to convey to all of us the reason why he came in the first place; namely, to reveal to us how much we are loved by God.

As I somewhat reluctantly leave this place, I realise yet again that the most difficult challenge for me lies in accepting the fact of my own belovedness. I know I have a lot of letting go and unlearning to do. Is it stretching even my sanctified imagination too far to really believe that I, too, can hear the faintest whisper borne on the breeze by the Jordan, 'This is my beloved daughter and I am pleased with her'? Before the pilgrimage is over, I will encounter the word 'beloved' again.

Moving on: we have come to Mount Tabor. The coach cannot negotiate the steep ascent so the rest of our journey is by taxi. Going up is not too much of a problem; going back down has us clinging on to each another! Our taxi driver has one hand on the steering wheel; in the other is his mobile phone. He conducts a spirited and prolonged conversation as we hurtle down a steep road with hairpin bends. Miraculously, we reach the coach park unscathed and, while we wait for the rest of the group to arrive in their taxis, I reflect on the experience of Mount Tabor. Scripture tells us it was a high mountain. That at least I can verify. Towering over the Plains of Megiddo and Jezreel Valley, and the ancient Via Maris, I can imagine how remote it would have been before the huge Church of the Transfiguration was built or the gardens laid out, or before modern transport made it relatively accessible. Jesus was seeking just such an isolated spot when he took his three companions, Peter, James and John, on a steep climb. I wonder how long it took them. It seems that the friends of Jesus were not allowed to remain too long in any one place, either internally or externally. They were continually being challenged out of their comfort zone. Jesus had such a short time, only three years, to teach, train and equip them to take the Good News to the ends of the earth. At this particular point they were being stretched by an encounter with a mystery that widened their horizons even further and took them into a deeper place of unknowing that, paradoxically, evoked within them an ancient recognition.

My first and lasting impression of Mount Tabor is one of deep stillness. There are crowds of pilgrims here from all over the world. There is much talk and bustle but this time it does not impinge on my consciousness. What arrests me is a sense of presence and awareness, as though I am on the cusp of encounter. The sense of the third dimension is more real than anything going on around me. All that is missing is the cloud, so pivotal in the faith journey of the ancient Israelites. For them, throughout all their wilderness wanderings, a cloud indicated the presence and glory of God and they believed that, when the longed-for Messiah would come, the cloud would once more descend, this time on the Temple. For now, the sky is an uninterrupted blue, with the sun blazing down. The 'then' becomes 'now' as I see in my mind's eye the three disciples keeping watch as Jesus moves away to pray. As they watch, it's as if they are on the very edge of the unseen world that becomes visible to them for a short time; as stated in Matthew 17, this is the moment known as the Transfiguration. The sun, for them, is Jesus' transfigured face and the dazzling white of his clothing.

And then, as if this isn't enough, the disciples' awe deepens as Moses, the greatest lawgiver, and Elijah, the greatest prophet in the history of the Jewish people, appear and engage in deep conversation with Jesus. It is no surprise that Peter breaks into this mystery, perhaps trying to fill the holy and other-worldly encounter with something because it's all too much for him. 'Lord this is wonderful! If you want me to, I will make three shrines, one for you, one for Moses, and one for Elijah.' He doesn't really know what he is saying; he has never experienced anything like this before. All he knows is that they have been let in on something very special and that it is good for them to be there. He wants to capture the moment, to remain on a high.

My friend interrupts my reverie. I know that her favourite feast day is the Feast of the Transfiguration and that she was greatly looking forward to her visit here. By tacit agreement we had left each other to our own reflections and wanderings around this beautiful place. She tells me that as she was gazing out over the Via Maris and prayerfully reflecting, someone approached her with the question, 'Are you a Catholic or a Protestant?' What could be more certain to bring someone who works for healing, reconciliation and peace in Ireland down to earth with a bang than this question, which also happened to come from another Irish person, and in such a setting? My friend is stunned and so am I. We expect such questions at home, but not here, not in this special place with the sense of the holy all around and the anticipation of the eternal breaking into time at any moment. Not here in this liminal place where I can reach out in my spirit and almost touch the unseen.

I have empathy with Peter's reluctance to leave. Up here, in this perfect stillness and the sense of presence, it would be so tempting to stay, while I know it's not possible for our group in practical terms. I think of some of the times when I have found myself on a spiritual high and would give almost anything to remain in that state, partly because what I am living in the everyday world just then isn't easy. Yet the mountaintop experience is always given in order to sustain us at the foot of the mountain when the going is tough, when we lose our way, when hope is at a low ebb, when pain threatens to crush us completely. The two experiences are part of the one reality of our journey of faith, as Peter discovered and as I am continually in the process of discovering. Luke tells us in his Gospel that Moses and Elijah were talking with Jesus about how he was about to fulfil God's plan by dying in Jerusalem. Perhaps in these moments Jesus was being given fresh courage and strength for what he knew lay ahead. I recall a descending cloud, coming down not on the physical Temple in Jerusalem but on the temple of Jesus' body, from which the disciples hear the voice of

God himself. 'This is my beloved son in whom I am well pleased. Listen to him.' As the cloud and the heavenly visitors disappear, the disciples cower in terror, but with the words 'Don't be afraid', they dare to look. They see 'only Jesus' – the Jesus they know and love and trust – the fully human being, beloved of the Father.

It's that word beloved again. I can't seem to escape it. It appears to represent something that is crucial for me, that I need to remember, that I have to appropriate for myself if I am ever going to authentically pass it on to others. And there are no shortcuts on this journey. I reflect that the literal meaning of transfiguration is a change in appearance. And transfiguration emanates from the process of being transformed. I can truly enter into such a process only when I know that I am the beloved. Otherwise it is too frightening. It is a challenge to leave my comfort zone and let go of what has been familiar and therefore safe, and choose to yield to love and the voice that calls. Once again I know that it is the only way. I look around at my travelling companions and know that as we meet again and again with Jesus, and as we begin to grow in the recognition that we are loved and special, staying open to the transforming power of the Spirit in our lives, our appearance, too, will change. People will sense that, in some mysterious way, we have been with Jesus and that it has been good for us to be there. We become more aware, more focussed. Old attitudes, old ways of behaving, inconsequential things (like whether we are Catholic or

Protestant, male or female, old or young, gay or straight), begin to fall away. More and more we see 'only Jesus' and 'only Jesus' can be seen in us.

As Jesus' three friends accompanied him down the mountain, they left the mystery but the mystery never fully left them. As they descended into what turned out to be a crisis that 'only Jesus' could address, namely the healing of a demon-possessed boy, they knew, in a place beyond their minds, that he was God's Messiah, the beloved Son. I sense it also, now that we are back in the valley, physically and spiritually, where loneliness or weariness or despair can often predominate. This is where I am called to be, the place where people ask excluding questions and seek to label others in order for them to cope with their own lives, or their denial that water is thicker than blood, or their ignorance of a common humanity, all beloved of Jesus. Perhaps true reality *is* up there on the mountaintop but, as we board the coach, I recognise, with the gift of awareness, that I am endlessly on the cusp of encounter with mystery, with 'only Jesus', this God-Man who I know as yet only a little but who always and ever calls me – and you – his beloved.

What does the phrase 'Water is thicker than blood'
call to mind for you?

Do you know yourself beloved?

A PRAYER

Lord, help me to see all those whom I encounter
this day and every day as my sisters, my brothers,
part of a common humanity,
loved by you.

And at those times when I feel overwhelmed,
help me to be still and to see 'only Jesus'. Amen.

CHAPTER ELEVEN

TREASURES OF DARKNESS

Dominus Flevit; Church of
Saint Peter in Gallicantu

(*Luke 19:41–46;*
Luke 22:54–62)

THERE IS A CHURCH ON THE MOUNT OF OLIVES DESIGNED
in the shape of a teardrop. Its name is Dominus Flevit – 'the
Lord weeps'. Somewhere in this area, on his final approach
to Jerusalem, Jesus paused and looked at the city spread
out in front of him, the Temple dominating its skyline.
He wept as he predicted the city's downfall. 'I wish that
even today you would find the way of peace, but now it
is too late and peace is hidden from you.' Our coach has
reached the Mount of Olives and we disembark for a first
look at the famous landmarks. Once again I can hardly
believe that we are actually here and I think everyone else
is feeling the same. I stand and I see not so much Jerusalem
as all the countries and cities it represents, especially my
own; all those places that have been shown the way to
peace but have turned from it. Is it too late for us? Is
peace hidden from us? Have we rejected too many God-
given opportunities? I find myself profoundly moved. In
humility, I am in communion with a God who weeps.

Fast-forward to the present, nearly four years since I was a traveller passing through the Holy Land. Over the past months I have, at times, felt myself transported back to that moment of communion when I found myself weeping over our 'Jerusalem'. Just as the Temple dominated the skyline of the Holy City so Belfast's skyline is dominated by the spires and steeples of churches of different persuasions. The Jewish people believed that the Temple was the special dwelling place of God and that it could not be destroyed, even though it had been reduced to rubble in 587 BC by Nebuchadnezzar the Great and the Babylonians. It was rebuilt but was to suffer a similar fate in AD 70 under the Roman general, later emperor, Titus. The Jewish people had not awakened to the fact that God cannot be contained in a building, however beautiful and sacred. They did not yet understand that his coveted dwelling place, his desired Temple, is in the hearts of humankind. More than two thousand years later, I am not sure if we fully understand, either. True, it is only now a small minority of the population that attends church and, while often feeling strong attachment to the building or the denomination, we do not have, for the most part, the equivalent powerful emotional ties to any one religious building as the Jews did to the Temple.

Having said that, the steady and unyielding drumbeat of sectarianism still manifests (or is interpreted as manifesting) itself in religious affiliation. It's as if we are stuck in a centuries-old mixture of denominational and political concrete, which has very little to do with the dwelling place of God, even though many invoke him as their champion. However, it has been heartening to recognise that there are still people of faith who have transcended that either/or approach, building on the wonderful legacy of so many different organisations, community groups and individuals. They have been, and continue to be, proactive in a courageous and humbling way, seeking to live the future we long for in the present moment by acting as image bearers of hope and peace. They are not, to put it mildly, popular in certain areas or among those whose agenda is far removed from the vision of a shared and peaceful future. It is convenient or easy to forget sometimes that Jesus, in his sojourn here on earth, was a Jew, faithful to the practices of his creed, fully conversant with the Scriptures; however, he was pointing beyond all of that, and beyond the Temple itself, to the loving relationship that God desires with each of us, without exception. Because his message of peace disturbed the religious and political power structures of his time, the Roman occupiers and the Jewish authorities sought to destroy Jesus. They had eyes but could not see. They had ears but could not hear. Peace was hidden from them, as it has been ever since.

But let us return to Dominus Flevit. We enter the 'teardrop' and are struck by the beauty of this little church. I am still in sombre mood. I am reminded of the fifteen wonderful Songs of Ascent (Ps 120–34) that pilgrims sang on their way to Jerusalem. I realise that the first one contains the verses, 'I am tired of living here among people who hate peace. As for me, I am for peace; but when I speak, they are for war.' And the penultimate Psalm begins, 'How wonderful it is, how pleasant, when brothers and sisters live together in unity.' It's almost as if the pilgrim has journeyed not only physically to this holy place but has reached a new way of seeing and of being. The final very short Song of Ascent is one of mutual blessing. The Psalms in between encapsulate much of what we experience on our spiritual journey. There are moments of awareness, moments of stillness when, like a child with its mother, we can rest content; moments of recognition of how God has rescued us, largely from our own folly, so that we escaped like a bird from the hunter's trap. There are times of waiting when we long for the Lord more than sentries long for the dawn. It is not to be wondered at that there are also many tears as we carry our individual and communal lament with us. But these are interlaced with moments of joy: 'Those who plant in tears will harvest with shouts of joy. They weep as they go to plant their seed, but they sing as they return with the harvest.' This journey that is paradoxically both an ascent and a descent holds for us more than we could ever imagine. In the wonderful words of the prophet Isaiah (45:3), God says, 'I will give you the treasures of darkness, riches stored in secret places, so that you will know that I am the God of Israel, the one who calls you by name.'

My mind wanders to another Psalm (137) that seems to sum up, more than I might care to admit, how I feel about so much that is going on in my own country and in the world. I wonder, as did the exiles of old, how we can sing the Lord's song in our strange world of war, oppression, greed, idolatry, injustice and fear. I look at the chalice window in the little church, symbol of both great love and great suffering, and leading to restoration. This window encompasses the whole world without exception and makes it possible to sing, to truly live the future we hope for in the present moment, all because of a God who weeps; all because of the 'blood of Christ shed for me, for you'.

On the front of the altar is a mosaic of a hen and her chicks. Somehow, in this sacred space, the words of Jesus over Jerusalem come alive in a new way, not just for this place but for everywhere. 'How often I have wanted to gather your children together as a hen protects her chicks beneath her wings' (Mt 23:37). The image assures me of the total protection, compassion, love and mercy of the God who still weeps and rejoices over a wayward and beloved creation. And I am able, at last, to pray for the peace not only of this Jerusalem but wherever our particular Jerusalem may be. I think I am also ready for whatever else Jerusalem may say to me.

First of all it was a hen and her chicks. Now it is a rooster! Perched on the dome of the Church of Saint Peter in Gallicantu (meaning the 'crow of the cockerel') on Mount Zion is a golden rooster, a permanent reminder of the night of Jesus' arrest and Peter's threefold denial of knowing him. We have come for a quiet time of reconciliation and also to reconnect with the traumatic events of those dark hours. It is thought that this may be where the house of the High Priest Caiaphas was located. After some time in this church, we descend via a stone staircase to an ancient cave or dungeon. There is no natural light. It is believed that in just such a bare, stark place Jesus would have been held prisoner. This was the place of no return. Ahead of him lay the unthinkable; the unimaginable. How alone he must have felt, how abandoned. Suddenly it all becomes very real to me. I have the urge to take off my shoes as a mark of respect, for this is surely holy ground. Seeking to shake off the all-pervading sense of foreboding and gloom, we climb back up and re-emerge into the sunshine of the courtyard.

In the courtyard is an amazingly lifelike sculpture with the inscription *Non novi illum* ('I do not know him'). Here is Peter, seated, leaning against a pillar, turning towards the servant girl with denial on his lips. Behind her is another challenger and, to Peter's right, a Roman soldier. Perched boldly atop the pillar is another rooster. In a holy 'flashback', I sense the drama of the interchange and Peter's fear and confusion, his impulsive reaction of self-preservation. Jesus had predicted that this would happen, only a few hours previously: 'Simon, Simon, Satan has asked to have all of you, to sift you like wheat.

But I have pleaded in prayer for you, Simon, that your faith should not fail. So when you have repented and turned to me again, strengthen and build up the others.' Peter had protested that this would never happen, that he was ready to go to prison with Jesus and even to die with him. And Jesus had responded, 'Peter, let me tell you something. The rooster will not crow tomorrow morning until you have denied three times that you even know me' (Lk 22:31–34). As I explained earlier in Chapter Two, it is this shadow side of Simon Peter's nature that would ultimately come to the fore that morning and result in that fateful denial. But the other side, the Peter in him, was still there, the Peter who would, as the first head of the Church, strengthen, nurture and build up the others. I have huge empathy with Peter. I know what fear can do. Jesus had only a short time earlier urged his friends to be of good courage. He had tried to warn them that they would need bucketloads of courage but they had no real conception of what lay ahead.

Having courage does not mean that we are not afraid. If we feel no fear, that is not courage. A better definition is perhaps the popular saying, 'Feel the fear and do it anyway.' The word 'courage' comes from the word 'heart' (from the French *coeur*). It denotes the way of the heart. With the mind, we work things out, rearranging, weighing up pros and cons, putting the necessary security cordons in place. I am not knocking the mind. It is an essential part of who we are, a huge, priceless, God-given gift. We cannot function without our minds. But what about the way of the heart? I don't mean sentimentality or emotionalism, but the hidden stirrings of almost inexpressible insights, urges, truths deep within us that we so often repress, either because we feel no one will understand or because we are afraid. I like the definition of wholeheartedness – to speak one's mind by telling all one's heart – this seems to me a good working partnership between heart and mind. To follow the way of the heart in this way seems like total abandonment and most of us are not really ready for that – yet! I recognise how often I resist, allowing caution to overrule the divine whisper. Peter was no coward. He felt the fear but didn't let it stop him following Jesus after his arrest to the High Priest's courtyard when most of the other disciples had fled in terror. He had experienced at first hand the teaching, healing, inclusive ministry of Jesus. He had felt the almost inexpressible urges, insights and truths stirring within him and he had even voiced some of them when the others couldn't. But faced with such a stark reality in that courtyard, he was being asked to express what he was not, as yet, all that sure of. Did he really know this man, Jesus? Or was some of what he had witnessed just wishful thinking on his part, surfacing out of a deep desire (along with that of countless of his fellow countrymen) for a Saviour, a Messiah? Surely if Jesus was the chosen one, any minute now he would show his hand, the scales would fall from his opponents' eyes, and all would be well. But Jesus spoke not a word. The silence screamed at Peter. So when he burst out with his denial, perhaps he was also saying, 'I don't know him. I thought I did, but now I'm confused. I don't know anything any more.'

I sense an element of this in Peter's denial. My thoughts are interrupted by our group starting to gather in a corner of the courtyard. Someone raises the first notes of the old spiritual, 'Were you there (when they crucified my Lord)'. We all join in this sacred moment, each with our own thoughts, as the haunting melody and challenging words ring out over the Kidron Valley. And I am there! I know what my own instincts for self-preservation can urge me to do and how my questions, confusion and uncertainties can cause me to miss the moment when things could have been so different. The rooster has crowed. I, too, am Peter.

But it doesn't end here. There was that look from Jesus straight at Peter, at me. It is not a look of condemnation but of love. At that moment, Peter remembered, with the anguish of searing regret. Later he would regard it as a treasure that came from darkness when, with that look, Jesus called him once again by name, and he knew beyond all doubt that Jesus was Lord and God. It was this look of love that finally broke Peter. For me, too, such a look would bring me to my senses faster than any word of judgement. Peter wept bitterly but this time it was the beginning of a turning back. They were redemptive tears. And Jesus still had to keep climbing, every step of that stone path, to the judgement seat of Rome on the

Via Dolorosa, the Way of Sorrows, to Calvary, where he 'climbed' the cross in that supreme act of love for all of humankind.

There's even more. As we leave this place, I cannot forget the rooster that heralds the end of darkness and the arrival of dawn. The rooster crowing was not simply or merely a reminder for Peter of his own weakness, of the Simon within him. It was a sign of hope; of a dawn about to break that no power of darkness would ever be able to extinguish. 'You are Peter and on this rock foundation – along with countless others – I will build my church.' Even before his final, supreme agony, anguish and dereliction, Jesus, in this moment, gave us the promise of a new day. As the eternal 'I Am', he gives us, even now, treasures of darkness, riches stored in secret places, so that we know and we believe, not because of anything we have done or failed to do but because of his loving faithfulness. So – let the rooster crow!

Can you spend some time praying one of the Songs
of Ascent (Ps 120–34)?

What treasures have you mined
from the darkness?

A PRAYER

Lord, let there be peace on earth,
and let it start with me.

And when I despair, keep me aware of the hope
that is always present because of you. Amen.

CHAPTER TWELVE

THE HARD
CHOICE

Gethsemane; Via Dolorosa

(*Matthew 26:36–49;*
Mark 15:21–24)

THERE CAN BE NO DOUBT WHATSOEVER THAT WE ARE IN
Jerusalem. First of all, there are crowds of people
everywhere, from every shade of Christianity, Islam
and Judaism. Second, all around, on every side, are the
familiar names and placenames that, unseen on this
pilgrimage until now, have coloured and given life to my
faith and journey. Perhaps none of these prompts me to
metaphorically take off my shoes more than does the
holy ground of the olive grove called Gethsemane. This
is where, for the final time, Jesus prayed and agonised
about what lay ahead for him if he were to fulfil his
purpose. And today we are here. The grove itself is more
meaningful for me than the large Church of All Nations
that borders it. We are not permitted to walk through
the garden, but there is a pathway around it, protected by
railings. Hundreds of pilgrims from every nation under
heaven are going in and out of the church yet, in the
midst of it all, I feel a strange quiet, almost a hush. Maybe

I am picking up on that sense of holy awe for which there is no adequate description.

What arrests my attention utterly are the olive trees, with their ancient, gnarled trunks. In an eternity moment, they appear to me to assume human form. In the church itself, in front of the altar, is the Rock of Agony on which Jesus prayed in deep distress, but here, outside the church, those events become real. They unfold themselves as I see the scene play out in the differing shapes of the tree trunks. There is Jesus pleading in prayer, in anguish, with his 'Father if it be your will let this cup pass me by.' A short distance away are the three disciples, falling asleep, worn out with confusion, grief and fear. Over there are the soldiers, the Temple Guard, among them some of the leading priests and rulers of Jerusalem. And here is Judas, stepping forward with his traitorous kiss of greeting.

I think again of the first recorded temptations of Jesus in the wilderness at the start of his public ministry. He wrestled with deciding which path to follow, but always returned to the bedrock of truth, as he knew it, in God. The Spanish poet Antonio Machado said, 'Walker, there is no road/The road is made by walking.'* Jesus made his path by walking – all the way to this olive grove and beyond. Matthew and Mark tell us that when the devil saw that he had not won the battle in the wilderness, he went away. Luke, however, says something different: 'The devil left Jesus until the next opportunity came' (Lk

4:13). And there were opportunities aplenty. After Peter's declaration that Jesus was the Messiah, for example, Jesus told his friends that the road he must walk would lead him to Jerusalem, to betrayal, trial and death, but that he would rise again. Peter, unbelieving, tried to dissuade him. This was the tempter speaking through one of his closest companions. Jesus rounded on him with the stark rebuke 'Get behind me, Satan. You are seeing things from a human point of view, not as God sees them' (Mt 16:23). There will have been many more such attacks that we are not told about in the Gospels, hidden in the Gospel narratives. Jesus was tempted in every way that we are. He didn't have a special escape route. He struggled as we do but did not give in.

I think of the many times in my life I have been faced with hard choices and how attractive, how alluring, the easier route can appear. I think of times when I have given in, either for more immediate gratification, because I am weary, or because I really do think that this is surely the best way. I am seeing things from a human point of view. But, thank God, there are other times, maybe not as frequent, when I make the hard choice. I realise that this is more due to the grace of God than to my inner strength, but gratitude flows when I realise that it is not so much that I am choosing but rather that the Way is choosing me. We can recognise and even feel encouraged by the wisdom, discernment and strength Jesus showed during the three years of his public ministry, but when it comes to Gethsemane, it's almost too much for us to contemplate; in fact, it is too much.

Looking at the olive grove, I allow myself to see what is no longer there, to be in that moment. I can hear Jesus say to his friends, 'Pray that you will not be overcome by temptation.' I realise the importance of the template for prayer that he gave us and, especially now, that deceptively simple phrase, 'Lead us not into temptation.' We are tempted every day, maybe even every hour, but with the caveat that we should not yield to it, should not give it houseroom lest it overcome us – the spirit is willing enough; the body is weak. Jesus had asked his friends to stay awake with him as he removed himself to a distance to pray. They fell asleep but we, centuries later, and within the eternal now of God, are silent witnesses of the gargantuan struggle that ensued here in this grove. It is a breathtaking mystery, a holy intimacy, as Jesus, in an agony of spirit so great that his sweat is like drops of blood, wrestles it out with God, but with each petition comes the submission, 'I want your will, not mine.' Even then, Jesus knew that he could call on his Father to send legions of angels to take him from this pit of indescribable agony, but no. 'Thy will be done on earth as it is in heaven.' I have never liked to rush my way through the Lord's Prayer, but I know that from now on I will pray it with even greater awareness and holy awe. For Jesus, the hard choice won through and this time it was final. There was no going back. The moment of his arrest was at hand.

And the cruel twist is that Jesus was identified by one of his own inner circle and betrayed by a kiss.

George MacLeod of Iona tells the story of the restoration of Iona Abbey and its furnishings. An artist was given the task of designing the communion goblets. Around the rim of each of the six beautiful plain-glass goblets were etched phrases from Scripture, five of them chosen by the Iona Community. The sixth phrase was left to the artist. He was an atheist but the words he chose were those of Jesus to Judas as he stepped forward to greet him in the Garden of Gethsemane as translated in the King James version of Matthew 26:50: 'Friend, wherefore art thou come?' – friend, why are you here? It's a deep, personal, intimate question. Still today I remember that story as clearly as if I had heard it yesterday instead of more than fifty years ago. And I hear it standing at the edge of this olive grove. Why am I here? My motives are often mixed. I can cover up a divided heart with nice words or actions. I may earnestly desire the best but sometimes I can think mine is the only way to follow, as I believe Judas thought, rather than 'Thy will be done on earth as it is in heaven.' Yet Jesus still called Judas, and still calls me, 'Friend'.

There is more for us to experience in this sacred place. Our guide tells us that the name 'Gethsemane' means 'olive press'; the press was used to squeeze the harvested fruit tightly in order to extract the oil. I am stunned. Why did I not know this before? The name of the grove is no accident. Here, Jesus' spirit was crushed and pressed almost beyond endurance, as he wrestled, in anguish, through to his *fiat*, to his 'Thy will be done'. I remember that the word 'anguish' comes from the Latin *angustus* meaning narrow or restricted. Anguish is the pain of a soul confined and restricted. Jesus' three friends could not bear to contend with the pain of a God who chose to be in such a place when he could have called on angels for protection. They slept, and darkness descended disguised as a kiss.

I think, on the macro level, of all the places in the world where so many are in anguish, confined and restricted due to the oppression, cruelty, greed or lust for power of others. I think, on the micro level, of the many individuals I have encountered who live an anguish beyond words, and I pray that they may know solidarity with the God who walks with them. I re-enter the Church of All Nations and recognise that the pilgrims are the first fruits of that anguish in the grove of the olive press and I pray for the courage to stay awake.

One of the things about this pilgrimage is that, while there is so much to see and to absorb that we almost feel overloaded, it is, at the same time, intensely personal and intimate. Each person has their own different expectations. Certainly, from our evening chats, it is clear that we have widely varying experiences of the same place. The stories of our pasts merge with the story of this journey to create for each of us an altered narrative of who we are and of what, or the one in whom, we believe. And even though our visits may not be in chronological order according to the Scriptures, for me, at least, they flow naturally and there is a sense of rightness about their sequence. This is true of what comes next. The Via Dolorosa.

In the Church of the Flagellation in the Muslim Quarter of the Old City is a graphic stained-glass window depicting the scourging of Jesus. After viewing this, we re-emerge soberly into the sunlight. This morning we are walking the Via Dolorosa, carrying a cross. Two of us are assigned to each Station of the Cross. As we pause at each Station, we pray and sing a verse of a psalm or hymn. The first surprise is that the choice of psalm allocated to the start of my stage is Psalm 23, the one from which we take our name, Restoration Ministries: 'He restores my soul.' The next surprise is when I discover that my Station, which I will perform with a fellow pilgrim, is the Fifth Station, 'Simon of Cyrene helps Jesus to carry his cross'. I find Simon of Cyrene one of the most intriguing characters in the Passion narrative. He had come from the countryside to celebrate Passover. His home was Cyrene, approximately 1,800 km away, so this was probably the trip of a lifetime for him. He had perhaps dreamt of it and planned it for years and at last he was here. However, on arriving in Jerusalem, it wasn't long before he was caught up in something that catapulted him right out of his comfort zone. We stop at the spot on the road where Roman soldiers often forced passersby to assist the condemned in carrying their crosses as they made the final ascent up the hill of crucifixion. I have always wondered about this man who appears only once in the Gospel narratives yet is written about as if he (or at least his children) was well known in the early Church – he is described as the father of Alexander and Rufus. There were no words spoken but something deeper was exchanged as Simon recognised that he was in the presence of someone very special. A final reluctant act of kindness for a condemned and dying man must have turned first into deep empathy and then great sorrow as he watched innocence, love, mercy and truth, in the person of Jesus, being nailed to a cross. The God of surprises was to make this journey to Calvary truly the journey of a lifetime for Simon, in a different way to what he had expected only a short time before. This, and not the Passover, as he had thought, was his reason for coming to the Holy City. The sacrament of encounter between Jesus and Simon of Cyrene signed and sealed Simon's destiny, namely, to be forever a follower of the one whose cross he bore.

The temptation is sometimes, maybe nearly always, to be lulled into some sense of 'This is the way things are going to be.' Then something happens. This could be a tragedy, or simply a change of circumstances or being in a particular place at a particular time, and our plans are lost. This is not the way we thought life would be. It's probably true to say that we are all, if not frightened, at least apprehensive when something that we haven't really planned for occurs. It leaves us feeling confused, uncertain, and wondering what the future holds. Yet, as people of faith, however stumblingly at times, we must know that we do not belong to ourselves. But if, or when, we resume our journey after our plans have been shattered, we may find that we are gradually being liberated into real life. This is what happened for Simon on that fateful day. It is what will continue to happen for us if we are faithful to the journey. When God arrests our attention, it may not initially seem like God. It can feel like a process of dying, and it is, in a way, because it is, yet again, the challenge to let go and let God in. It's not easy. It calls for great trust and surrender. Like so much else, it is a process. We all experience hard times on our journey through life. While God does not will suffering upon us, when such suffering does occur, it may be that the God of surprises has planned something for us that is far more perfect than we could ever have imagined or even hoped for. Our response can be to say 'Amen!' Simon's 'amen' was initially forced out of him but it became, in the end, an enormous gift.

As I pause, reflecting, at the Fifth Station, I notice a hollow indentation in the ancient wall that borders the narrow street. It is unmistakeably the imprint of a hand. Tradition has it that as Jesus stumbled on the way to his crucifixion, he put out his hand to steady himself. Down through the centuries, pilgrims have followed this route and placed their hands on this imprint in solidarity with their Lord, over time hollowing it out. I do the same. In a flash, I see a succession of hands; the hands of soldiers who rough-handled the prisoners and the reluctant Simon, and who later would hammer nails into agonised limbs; the hands of Simon who helped bear the weight of the cross, with each step along this Way of Sorrows becoming increasingly aware of the one his hands were helping; most of all, the hands of Jesus, hands that had healed and embraced and blessed, so soon to be pierced by cruel nails. I look at my own hands and know that I am part of an endless succession of humankind, including those soldiers and Simon, who are forgiven, healed and blessed by those hands nailed to a cross on Calvary. And I pray that my hands may always be used to welcome, reconcile and bless.

And so to 2022: for months now, due to the COVID-19 pandemic, we have not been allowed to use our hands in these ways. It has not been possible to hug anyone, or simply clasp another's hand without words, because the most effective way to communicate your depth of feeling to another is to hold or grip their hand. I have really missed this. This sacrament of touch may be denied us, but thinking back to the grove of the olive press and Simon and the Way of Sorrows and the handprint, we can still find ways to clasp one another in love and for love, because of the one who made the road by walking it, who made the hard choice so that humankind might defeat the virus of separateness and find itself (or be found) once again as the beloved community.

---

* Antonio Machado, 'Proverbs and Songs' in Willis Barnstone (trans.), *Border of a Dream: Selected Poems of Antonio Machado* (Port Townsend, Washington: Cooper Canyon Press) p. 281.

Can you take time to remember a period of hard
choices, of struggle, in your life?
What did it feel like? After remembering, can you
pray the Lord's Prayer aloud slowly?

Think of a time when you reached out your hand
in faith and generosity. Were there any surprising
consequences?

A PRAYER

Lord, there is so much anguish in the world that
I am often tempted to fall asleep because I feel
powerless to do anything about it. Keep me awake
to what you would have me see.

May my hand always leave the imprint of
friendship, inclusion and welcome. Let me leave
one such imprint today. Amen.

CHAPTER THIRTEEN

BEAUTIFUL
FEET

Room of the Last Supper;
Site of the Ascension

(John 13; Acts 1:1–11)

WE ARE STILL IN JERUSALEM, THIS TIME IN THE UPPER
Room (or *Cenacle*, from the Latin for dining room).
Whether this location is truly the site of both the Last
Supper and where the followers of Jesus gathered to pray
after the Resurrection is under question. To my mind,
this is not as important as the memories of events that
such a room brings to mind. The room is large enough
to hold the 120 believers mentioned in the Acts of the
Apostles. I allow my 'sanctified imagination' free range
and, in doing so, sense something of the conflicting
emotions played out in that room (or one very like it)
during a few short weeks nearly two thousand years ago,
the fear and the sadness, the confusion, the remorse
and the grief, the incredulity, the excitement, the joy,
the peace, the love – and the wonder of the Pentecost
visitation.

I see disciples and friends of Jesus sharing in the
Passover meal that will become, forever after, the

template for the Eucharist. I do sense, in my spirit, that there were women here as well as men. Women formed a crucial part of his inner band of followers and some of them were with him right to the end when the men had run away. It is only natural that they are here, albeit probably fulfilling their traditional role of waiting at table. They understand and know instinctively how to serve. I see Jesus, modelling for his friends the sort of servant leadership he wants them to exercise as he washes their feet, a task normally reserved for the lowest slave. Their stunned silence when he begins to kneel is broken, of course, by Peter, who always blurts out what the rest of them are thinking but can't say. 'Lord you will never wash my feet!' Jesus' response, 'If I don't do this you have no place with me', even at this emotionally charged moment, challenged not only Peter and his fellows but all of us to rethink what it means to call ourselves friends, followers, or image bearers of Jesus. 'If I your Lord and Teacher have washed your feet, you ought to wash each other's feet. I have given you an example to follow. Do as I have done to you. How true it is that the servant is not greater than the master. Nor are messengers more important than the one who sends them. You know these things – now do them. This is the path of blessing.'

I reflect that this is one of the hidden Beatitudes in the Gospels: 'Blessed are you when you wash one another's feet.' I think of how often in the history of the Church, servants or messengers have communicated an image of importance, power and authority. We have allowed our smaller selves, our egos, to dominate and have not understood the truth that liberation into the realm of our true selves depends, at least in part, on our willingness and ability to let go, to unlearn what we thought was so important, indeed vital, to our survival, our calling. When, or if, we achieve such an awakening, we see that the answer was there all along in the form of the servant king who eternally kneels before us, raising us up into a knowledge of who we really are, the beloved daughters and sons of God. By washing the feet of his friends, he invites us to citizenship of a kingdom whose charter consists of the Beatitudes, both overt and hidden, that we find in the Gospels. And this particular path of blessing surely ranks among the most important.

I am arrested again by the shadows I feel in the room. I listen in to the conversation around the table and among others who are not seated. There is tension in the air and attempts made to cover it over by filling some of the silences. I see the act of betrayal put into operation. Jesus hands Judas the choicest morsel, a sign of friendship and honour, as if he seeks to draw this man back from the brink. Judas disappears into the shadows, goes out into the night, to execute a deed that can only be done under cover of darkness. As so often before, I reflect on how easy it is for me to make Judas into the scapegoat; history has made him into the ultimate pariah. This scapegoating can be a sort of avoidance, an attempt to banish the thought that there is some of Judas in all of us, certainly in me. While not condoning his action for one moment, I know there are times when I have chosen to judge or criticise another whose behaviour, so I think, fails to measure up to the standards of a friend of Jesus. But if I pause there and seek to be courageous enough to look at myself, I can see that the things I most heatedly accuse others of are precisely some of the same shadows that I identify within myself. It is always painful to reach such recognition, but it can be redemptive as well. I know I am a slow learner but I am also glad of this awakening. Judas awakened too late and it was his bitter remorse that killed him. The others would experience grief and regret, as I do, but these emotions, rather than leading to destruction and death, led and continue to lead to a greater knowing and, hopefully, a greater freedom.

Again, in this room of shadows, I sense Peter's protestations of loyalty and Jesus' response. I hear some of what Jesus said in farewell, wonderful things like, 'Love one another as I have loved you. There is no greater love than to lay down your life for your friends. You are my friends' (Jn 15:12–14). Or 'Do not be afraid. I have overcome the world' (Jn 16:33). Or 'You are sad now, you will mourn and weep, but in a little while you will be filled with gladness' (Jn 16:20). I feel sad that Jesus cannot share with them all that is in his heart because he knows that they could not bear it. And I want to cry out to him, 'What is it, Lord, that you feel we could not bear?' I pause and am reduced to wonder and awe as I remember that in this room, or one like it, Jesus prayed for his friends who were with him. But he prayed not only for them; he prayed for all those who would ever believe because of their witness. That means me and the people around me and a vast host from every age. In the eternal now of God, Jesus is praying for us. Not only is he praying that we will all, in our marvellous diversity, be united in love, but much more importantly that we might be one as he and the Father experienced such unity, an inner unity that moves beyond an either/or mentality into a consciousness of that spiritual dimension of beloved community where everything belongs. That, and not an external uniformity, is what will enable and convince a broken, weary, anguished, conflicted world to believe.

I look again at this room. It is from such a room that Jesus went out into the shadows of betrayal, anguish, denial and all that followed after his arrest in Gethsemane. In such a room his followers hid behind locked doors in fear and trembling. Into such a room Mary Magdalene came running three days later with the incredible message: 'Christ has died; Christ is risen; Christ will come again.' Into such a room he came, that same day, with his greeting of *Shalom*, of resurrection, and of commission. In such a room his friends, both women and men, watched and prayed, and from such a room they would leave, walking on the same feet he washed before his death, bringing the good news of peace to Jerusalem,

Judea, Samaria and the ends of the earth. Because of their witness, we are standing here today.

The figures fade and the shadows recede. I look around at our little group, also all followers, friends of Jesus, each one as different from the other as they were long ago and I realise once more that what unites us is so much more than what would seek to divide us. Whether we fully recognise it or not, we are the body of Christ; we are already one in the Spirit. No matter what obstacles the locked doors of our own or other people's making may present, he emerges from the shadows. And his greeting is always and ever, 'Peace be with you.'

We move from Mount Zion to the Chapel of the Ascension on the Mount of Olives and soon find the spot that commemorates Jesus' ascension into heaven. In terms of our faith journey, the Ascension really marks the end of one chapter and the beginning of another. In a few days' time, through the coming of the Holy Spirit, the friends of Jesus are empowered, just as he promised, to be his witnesses to the ends of the earth. They, too, leave the Upper Room, as we did. I have an image of an unstoppable energy spiralling outwards through Jerusalem, Judea, Samaria and the endless beyond. The fruit of that energy is evident in the fact that people from the 'ends of the earth' have come to this holy land throughout the centuries to see where it all began. This site is now under Islamic jurisdiction but, on the Feast of the Ascension, the different Christian traditions are allowed to celebrate here. I find myself wondering, as so often before, why they cannot unite and celebrate together, something that would witness good news afresh to the ends of the earth and create a renewed energy. I do not find much here to arrest my attention.

Then, suddenly, I see the footprint. I wouldn't have noticed it unless it had been specifically pointed out. Tradition has it that this is the footprint of Jesus, the point from which he ascended into heaven. Actually, it doesn't even look like a footprint, more just an indentation in the rock. But the concept behind it captures my imagination. I remember that Luke tells us that the risen Jesus took his followers to Bethany, a village at the foot of the Mount of Olives. The name Bethany means 'house of welcome'. One house in particular was Jesus' safe place, where he felt at home, accepted and loved; the house of Mary, Martha and Lazarus. It seems fitting that it is here that Jesus chose to say farewell. Implicit in his goodbye was this challenge to his followers to go and spread the good news of the restored hospitality between humankind and God, between the alienated parts of their own inner beings, between themselves and others who are different; hospitality with the whole created order restored.

Before leaving, Jesus told his disciples to wait in Jerusalem until the Holy Spirit came. It is salutary to realise how often the invitation, or command (as it was in this case), to wait crops up in the Gospels. The natural impulse is usually to be up and doing and this can be the right thing to do sometimes but at others it is just a waste of energy if we have not first waited and listened for what God is doing. Then we can join in. In this case, the disciples were to wait for the gift of the Spirit who would empower and energise them to do what God had planned. I reflect on how difficult I find it at times to know when to wait and when to go. But I also realise that, at crucial points of decision in my life, after waiting has come a moment when, almost suddenly, I simply got up and went! Let's fast-forward to this hard time of pandemic. What a long time we have been given to wait! Perhaps the summons will come soon with an invitation to step over the threshold into a different world, even for those of us who are getting old, if we still have pilgrim souls. What have we experienced in our waiting? And how can we, in this moment, act as witnesses to Jesus to the ends of the earth? I am immediately conscious of those I know who have already done exactly that. I think of different places where they have taken the welcome of Jesus to many. They have been a 'Bethany' through their commitment to community, shared prayer and hospitality. And they have done it not in their own strength but empowered by the Spirit.

I return to my fellow pilgrims and I look at their feet. I look at my own. Where have these feet been? What stories could they tell? I give thanks for the wonder of having feet that take me from one place to another. These feet have brought me to the Holy Land and will take me back to Ireland with new stories, hopes and dreams to share. I remember again the words of the poet/prophet Isaiah of Jerusalem, 'How beautiful on the mountains are the feet of those who bring good news of peace.' Friends of mine in the United States have a nickname for me; they call me 'Beautiful Feet'; I suppose because of the work of peaceful reconciliation we seek to do in Restoration Ministries. I don't feel I deserve it, but receive it in the spirit in which it is offered. I have another friend in Brazil who says, 'Where your feet are, there will your head be too.' It's maybe another way of saying, as did Matthew, 'Where your treasure is, there will your heart be also' (Mt 6:21). What I think my friend really means is, 'Where your feet have walked, that is where your commitment, your passion, your calling, your energy, will be.' In this moment I give thanks for all the unknown beautiful feet down through the ages that have made a path by walking, that have walked courageously through discord and war in this holy land and in my own land and many others, bringing a message of a different road that may be travelled. They are the feet of the reconcilers, the peacemakers, the bearers of hope; those who are carriers of forgiveness, of openness, of welcoming diversity; of letting go of those parts of the past that imprison in order to be awake to the present moment and to embrace the future. They are the feet of those who have not remained gazing up into heaven but have sought to be image bearers of Jesus here and now. I ask myself, 'What imprint have my feet left? Are my feet "beautiful"?'

From the site of Jesus' ascension to the year 2022: dear reader, can I invite you, as someone invited me some years ago, to take a moment to look at your feet and ask yourself, 'Where have these feet been? Among whom have they walked? What vision has been catapulted from these feet to my heart and head because of where they have walked?' Thank God for every occasion when your feet have carried the good news of peace to different places and people, for your feet that have made a road by walking, for your feet that have enabled you to be present to others, to share their hopes, their anguish and their struggles. Thank God for all you have been enabled to be and give and do. Now look again at your feet. For those of you who are older, perhaps you feel that these feet can't carry you very far any more. But where you cannot physically go, you can go in another way, through prayer. It is a priceless resource and one to which we need to awaken more deeply. I thank God for your feet that are now treading the path of prayer and of lovingly listening to the sorrows of the world. And for those of you who are young, who are able still to run and not grow weary, thank God for the wonder of being able to take the good news of peace, of unity in diversity, of belonging to each other, to a world that aches to hear. I thank God for you, also. Truly you have beautiful feet.

The civil rights icon Rosa Parks is reputed to have
said, 'My feet is tired, but my soul is marchin'!'
Where have your feet taken you?
Is your soul still marching?

A PRAYER

Dear Lord, I pray for the Church, the Body of
Christ. May all that is good that is still imprisoned
in the shadows of fear or caution or control emerge
into the light of your presence so that the world
may be blessed.

And may my feet always be guided into
the ways of peace. Amen.

CHAPTER FOURTEEN

AWAKENING

Church of the Holy
Sepulchre; Abu Ghosh

(*Luke 24:1–34*)

ON THIS, THE LAST DAY OF OUR PILGRIMAGE TOGETHER,
dear reader, I wonder how the journey has been for you,
whether you have been encouraged along the way. The
word that comes to mind is 'awakening', an experience
that does not just happen once but happens many, many
times throughout life. I hope, as we have travelled together
through the Holy Land of Scripture and also the holy
land of our own spirits, that you will have had moments
of awakening. I know, as I have shared with you, that
I have been blessed with such moments at unexpected
times. And so, shall we get back on our metaphorical
coach for our final visits?

We are back in the Old City of Jerusalem at the Church
of the Holy Sepulchre in the Christian Quarter. This vast
area marks the location of the crucifixion, burial and
resurrection of Jesus. It is called one of the holiest and most
venerated places on earth. Ever since the fourth century
AD it has been a place of pilgrimage for countless millions

of people. I am somewhat bewildered; there is so much noise and bustle and this time I cannot move beyond it. People are praying, sweeping floors, taking photographs, shouting to one another in different languages. There are tour guides who have lost some of their party. There are other pilgrims who abandon any attempt at an orderly queue in their haste and determination to get to the place of crucifixion, where they will kneel and stretch out their hands to touch the hole where the vertical beam of the cross is supposed to have been hammered into position. I feel empathy with Mary Magdalene who, on that first Easter morning, cried to someone she assumed to be the gardener, 'They have taken away my Lord and I don't know where they have put him.' I feel that I cannot find him, either. I look at the faces of those milling around me, some excited, some angry, some awestruck, some prayerful, and immediately feel a pang of guilt, because I think that here, in this place above all others, I should be able to sense something!

I look again at the hundreds of people, all with their own stories and life histories and different reasons for being here. I remember that in the ancient world this site lay outside the walls of Jerusalem, on a busy cosmopolitan route. Here soldiers kept watch, gambling away the time perhaps partially to dull their senses to the agony going on around them. Among the crowds were the morbidly curious, the spectacle seekers, the scoffers and the self-righteous, as well as the pious from the different religious sects to whom Jesus had been a threat. But here, too, were those who believed that Jesus was the Messiah, the Saviour of the world. Here was his mother, now experiencing to the full the sorrow that was predicted would pierce her heart like a sharp sword, and Mary Magdalene and a group of women who were numbered among his closest friends. In such a place he died. Among such as we he breathed his last. Now is really no different from then. As I think of this, yesterday and today merge into one. And if that is so, then here he was anointed for burial and entombed. Here, too, he is risen.

In my mind's eye, I return to that first Easter. It's very early in the morning and three women are making their way to the tomb into which the body of Jesus was placed a couple of days before. Sealed behind a huge stone lay all their hopes and dreams. Who were they now – without him? Ever since their first encounter with him, Jesus had given them a new way of looking at life, of being and thinking and acting. He had revealed to them the truth of who they really were – beloved daughters and sons of God. And that truth rang true to the very core of their beings. How quickly such conviction faded! If there was any remembrance at all, it was in the form of a lament for what had been and would be no more. Jesus was dead so what was left to give their lives meaning? Clinging to the last shreds of what had been, they were going to anoint his dead body when it suddenly hit them that they would not be able to roll away the boulder from the entrance.

They didn't have the physical strength. They arrived at the place, which would have looked so different then than it does today – I don't even know where I'm supposed to be looking. Instead I return in my imagination to the beloved story I know so well. I see again what's not there. I see the three women stopped in their tracks by the amazing sight of a clear entrance to the tomb. Someone had got there before them. Who?

Startled and fearful, they entered what they expected to be darkness, only to find sitting there a person, clad in a white robe, who addressed them directly: 'Do not be surprised. You are looking for Jesus the Nazarene who was crucified. He isn't here! He has been raised from the dead! Look, this is where they laid his body.' I wonder what message they heard and held on to. If they were anything like me, probably all they heard was 'He isn't here!' The ultimate cruelty; they weren't even given the chance to anoint his body, the only thing left for them to do for him. Who had disposed of the corpse? So conditioned are they to a two-dimensional world where someone was alive and now is dead that it prevents them from hearing the alternative message that changed everything. He is risen! He is not here. He is risen.

Sometimes I think we live our lives as if there is still an enormous stone to roll away. I know I do; I even create these stones for myself! I allow doubt or fear or despair or grief to overtake me, blocking my way forward and threatening to become as insurmountable as that boulder. I think it's because I focus sometimes on the problem rather than being still and recognising that I'm not going to be able to shift it; letting go is the only way, thus giving God the freedom to act. Once again it's all about trust. I also reflect that much of our witness, as the Church, could appear to outsiders like people living in the past, going to worship as if they were going to anoint a dead body. There is little sense of a God who has risen and who, vibrant and alive, is coming to meet with us. There is little expectancy. And we leave, or switch off, maybe with a feeling of disappointment because he isn't here. We haven't been permitted to anoint his dead body. We don't expect to witness eternity breaking into time in the form of a heavenly messenger. The God of surprises hasn't shown up for a long time and so we go through the motions of hankering after the past, going back to what is familiar, to a way of doing things that is probably not always comfortable but was the world we knew.

Actually, those three women had set out on their journey that morning seeking closure to the trauma that had thrown their lives into chaos and despair. They didn't know it then, but they were instead walking towards the future. Not only was the entrance to the tomb open, but a door had also been opened to the unseen world that would never again be closed. I hear again the words spoken by the messenger, 'Why are you looking for the living among the dead? He is not here! He is risen!' 'He is not here' can either feed our despair or cause us to lift up our hearts with excitement, expectation and joy! Earlier at this sacred site I, too, was looking in the wrong place, looking for the living among the dead stones of yesterday. He is not there. But he is here, among these pilgrims, these living stones. And I know that he is risen every time a person opens their heart in faith. This *is* a holy place. And not only that, my courage and expectancy increase as I remember that it is these women who run into the future with the first commission to proclaim the news of resurrection; of new life, of hope, of freedom.

As if to reinforce the message, we are back on the coach, being taken the short distance from Jerusalem to Abu Ghosh, possible site of the first-century village of Emmaus. In Luke's Gospel we are told that it was about seven miles from Jerusalem. As we drive along, I try to get beyond the modern streets and buildings and see, instead, a dry and dusty road with just the occasional traveller. Along this road two people are walking, Cleopas and his companion, whom I have always felt was his wife, Mary (one of those who had stood at the foot of the cross along with Mary Magdalene and Mary the mother of Jesus). They are going home after the harrowing event of the Crucifixion. They find it hard to put one foot in front of the other. The mantra of their journey is 'We had hoped.' Their unseen companions are fear, grief and despair. Their world, which such a short time before seemed open to endless possibilities, full of hope and awareness of that third dimension which characterises vibrant faith, has shrunk to a two-dimensional existence from which all hope has disappeared.

So enveloped are they in their grief that they fail to notice that someone has silently joined them on the road. Perhaps initially they are annoyed. But the stranger opens up a conversation by asking a seemingly innocent question that heralds a whole new awakening. Their journey gradually becomes transformed as he alerts them to a new understanding of Scripture. It is now as if, with each step, they are moving into a deeper and deeper insight in relation to the events they have been living over recent turbulent days. They are being stretched. With dawning awareness, they begin to see things differently and hope enters their despair. Later they will say of this experience that their hearts were strangely warmed, as if burning within them. By now they are nearly at the village of Emmaus and, when they reach their house, they are so taken with their new companion and the way he has gently changed their way of seeing that they press him to come in and stay with them. I love the old translation of their words of invitation and welcome, 'Abide with us for it is toward evening and the day is far spent.' We are familiar with what happens next in this, one of the most beloved of resurrection stories. In the sharing of a meal, in the blessing and the breaking of the bread, they are awakened; they know now that 'It is the Lord!' They leave their meal untouched and run back, transformed, to

Jerusalem, the place they had left such a short time before in fear and despondency.

I fast-forward to the present, this now, and I think what an appropriate and encouraging prayer that invitation given to the Lord by Cleopas and Mary is for those of us who are elderly. We have journeyed far, both in terms of physical distance and in terms of our spiritual understanding. Truly for us it is now toward evening and the days of our lives are far spent. Our prayer, too, is 'Abide with us Lord, stay with us.' The word 'abide' strikes me again with its deep sense of indwelling, of the hospitality of our spirits. We know the journey ahead is filled with mystery, perhaps more so than at any other point in our earthly lives. Yet at the heart of mystery is the dwelling place of God. Jesus had left them physically but Cleopas and Mary had a new and outrageous hope. Out of a sense of abiding, they were able to run with expectancy and joy. Running seems to characterise most of the resurrection accounts, running not with panic and fear but with outrageous hope. It is my prayer that both you, dear reader, and I, when the time comes, may run untrammelled and with that same outrageous hope into eternity.

I return to the end of our pilgrimage, an ending that can also be a beginning. I am in the Church of the Resurrection at Abu Ghosh/Emmaus. I reflect on the importance of journeying. I look around at my fellow pilgrims. True, we have physically travelled much farther than Cleopas and Mary. Soon we will be returning home to Ireland. What were our expectations when we set out? How has our way of seeing changed? What has opened up for us so that we will never again think the same about some of the Scripture we thought we knew completely? We have broken bread together on many occasions, both at mealtimes and in the Eucharist. Have our hearts burned within us as we shared friendship and food and recognised Jesus present among us in the 'now' that has been so special? We travel home by the same route, but on our inner pilgrimage, what is new? What fresh awakening gives our spirits wings? Can we say deep within our beings, 'It is the Lord!'?

As our pilgrimage draws to a close,
what will you remember?

A PRAYER

Forgive me, Lord, for so often seeking the living
among the dead. Help me instead to open
myself up to your risen presence, you who are
continually calling into being those parts of me
that are lifeless.

You are a pilgrim, God. Thank you for
companioning us on this unforgettable
pilgrimage. Amen.